Friends and Foes
in the Transkei

DESCENT INTO THE KEI VALLEY

Friends and Foes in the Transkei

A Victorian lady's experience of
Southern Africa during the 1870's

Helen M. Prichard

LEONAUR

Friends and Foes in the Transkei:
A Victorian lady's experience of
Southern Africa during the 1870's
by Helen M. Prichard

First published under the titles
Friends and Foes in the Transkei

Leonaur is an imprint
of Oakpast Ltd

Copyright in this form © 2009 Oakpast Ltd

ISBN: 978-1-84677-758-5 (hardcover)
ISBN: 978-1-84677-757-8 (softcover)

http://www.leonaur.com

Publisher's Notes

In the interests of authenticity, the spellings, grammar and place names
used have been retained from the original editions.

The opinions of the authors represent a view of events in which he
was a participant related from his own perspective,
as such the text is relevant as an historical document.

The views expressed in this book are not necessarily
those of the publisher.

Contents

To

MADAME LA COMTESSE DE LA TAILLE DES ESSARTS,

AND TO

MADAME LA BARONNE D'ARLHAC,

THIS LITTLE VOLUME IS DEDICATED,

IN

MOST AFFECTIONATE REMEMBRANCE OF MY HAPPY
VISIT TO VERSAILLES.

Preface

This work is compiled from rough notes, diary, and private letters written to personal friends. The writer hopes that what has proved interesting to her own circle may not be deemed altogether unworthy of perusal by the greater world composed of those who take an interest in the late events, in South Africa. Although the details of the campaign have been already ably and powerfully presented to the public by the pens of our special correspondents, yet there are many links in the chain of events which immediately preceded the war, that can only be supplied by those who were on the spot at that time. As Mrs. Prichard was in the Transkei for some time before the advance of the Imperial troops took place, she ventures to lay her personal experiences of our "Friends and Foes," before the public.

CHAPTER 1

Arrival at Table Bay

On the 13th of May, 1876, I arrived with my husband at Table Bay, Cape of Good Hope; accompanied by our only child, a little boy two years and a half old.

A few weeks later my husband received instructions from Government to proceed at once to the Umtata a remote district about one hundred, miles beyond the eastern frontier, and as circumstances concurred to prevent my accompanying him, I was left for ten dreary months, in perhaps the most trying position in which a woman can be placed; and I never recall that lonely, weary time at the Cape without a shudder!

However, as time went on, I was fortunate in gaining many steadfast and faithful friends, whose kindness I remember with the brightest and warmest recollection, and whose prosperity and happiness will always give me pleasure.

During this period another dear little son was sent to comfort me, but his delicate health proved an additional source of anxiety, and I was indeed thankful when a telegram from my husband heralded his speedy arrival, as my baby was in a most critical state, and I much feared the gentle, patient spirit would quit the fragile little body before his father had looked upon his sweet face.

However, he rallied, and was sitting upon my lap, playing with his tiny toys, when (on my husband's birthday, the 29th May, 1877), baby's nurse, my good Kitty, threw open the door, and in a would-be dignified, but very excited and happy voice, announced my husband as if he were a stranger! Little Henry, who had been promoted to knickerbockers since Papa went away, stood gazing at the sunburnt visitor rather suspiciously; and I think we all felt a little shy (as people are apt to do after long partings), and a little confused as to what to speak of first, where there was so much to say and hear.

I thought the best thing we could do was to go out for a long walk, which ended in a luncheon with Colonel Lanyon (then Administrator of Griqualand West), at Cogill's Hotel, next door to Drake's boarding house, where we were staying.

After lunch, my husband and I had a charming drive through the pretty environs of Wynberg, paying farewell visits to our friends and arranging a programme which would enable us to accomplish all that had to be done before starting for the Transkei, which we hoped to do in about ten days.

Pardon my dwelling so long upon this happy day, one of the brightest in my life!

It was so delightful to feel cared for again, and to have no more solitary walks to face, that I venture to hope my gentle readers may bear patiently with me: and I do not write for those who are not gentle.

War and its horrors will follow fast enough! prosaic packing and practical preparation for a rough frontier life; and I claim some excuse for lingering lovingly over my last sunbeam, my idle, merry, happy day, which preceded days of hard work, and nights of anxious thought; bracing myself for the hardships of the rough future which lay before me, and wondering if I could really be useful in a life for which my education had so little fitted me.

My friends too, were rather too bad, in warning me about all the horrors I had to expect! One lady informed me she had frequently been compelled to cut up a sheep with her own hands! and I could not imagine myself in the character of a butcher! though willing to turn baker occasionally. But these stories did not alarm me so much as the gentle kindness and suggestions offered by those who really felt for me; and I eagerly welcomed every scrap of information to enable me somewhat to picture and prepare for this strange, weird Kafirland, to which I resolutely turned my face, and in which I hoped to make a happy home for my husband and children.

There was some delay in receiving instructions from Government, and we did not start on our long journey until the 6th July, when we took leave of our kind friends at Drake's, and drove off in a Cape cart to the Docks.

This Cape cart is an invention admirably adapted for keeping the feet cold, and the head hot! beyond these advantages I see few others, and these are rather questionable! It certainly bears a distant family-likeness to a French *char-à-bancs*, and also to the ubiquitous American buggy, but is evidently looked upon as a poor relation, possessing neither the comfort of one nor the elegance of the other. However, the uncomfortable Cape cart reigns supreme in South Africa, and into one we were compelled to climb on this July morning no English July, remember, but the first month of the Cape winter. A raw Scotch mist, soon turned into equally raw rain, succeeded by blazing sunshine, which finally ushered in a furious south-easter.

At the docks we met a certain Mrs. Gog, whom I had engaged a few days before as nurse, and who subsequently became quite a celebrity in the Transkei. I was most anxious that Kitty should accompany us, but a sweetheart objected (naturally) to her departure, and of course I had to submit! For weeks I sought in vain for a suitable person to replace her, and was almost in despair when a knock at my door announced a lady in an Ulster, who described herself as Johanna Gog!!

At first sight the idea of anything so rough-looking even touching my little Granville occurred to me as so inexpressibly ludicrous that I could scarcely repress a smile; but a moment's consideration reminded me that rough people suited rough places, and that this hard-looking personage might make an invaluable house-cleaner or cook when we arrived at our Kafir home, while she could not hurt the little one *en voyage*, as he would be under my own eye night and day.

So I admitted her into the room, where she proceeded to make herself at home by instantly seating herself upon an ottoman, which, happening to be lower than the chairs her ladyship was accustomed to rest her fair weight upon, drew from her a smothered exclamation which amused me immensely. She then took off a pair of black kid gloves (gentleman's size) with which she wiped her face said the heat made her "quite faint," and commenced fanning herself with the beforementioned gloves, which seemed capable of making themselves useful in any capacity!

I thought the owner of such gloves might prove a treasure; and as closer inspection satisfied me that she was enormously strong, and had a clever face, I decided to humour her a little and not take offence at her colonial airs.

She then informed me that a lady-friend of hers had told her that an English person, named Mrs. Prichard, wanted a nurse to go to the fields.

"That's the woman for me, says old Johanna" (I merely quote), "so I got my sister to drive me out in the cart, and thought I would come and see how I liked you, mum!"

This was' rather reversing the usual order of things; but as one knows the very stars are upside down in South Africa, I was not much surprised, and I rather enjoyed the idea of trying to tame this quaint specimen, and converting her into a respectable servant. I told her that we were not bound for the Fields, but for the Transkei that is to say, Kafirland beyond the frontier, and not in the colony at all.

"Shall you go in the post-cart? "she inquired.

"No! Partly by sea, in a comfortable steamer; then by train; and, finally, in the wagon which Government has placed at my husband's disposal."

"Oh, that's first-rate," she replied.

She then favoured me with a graphic description of the miseries of the post-cart, and of the amusing way in which passengers converted themselves into portmanteaux, by wearing the greatest quantity of apparel they could possibly contrive to put on, in order to baffle the regulations as to amount of luggage permitted!

My husband's entrance fortunately put a stop to this harangue, which threatened to branch off into a family history of her various relatives; charming people, no doubt, but not quite relevant to the subject in hand!

Edward promptly recalled her to the practical question of wages, when she, as promptly, demanded twelve pounds a month! (modest) but naively hinted that "she would come for much less!"

This reminded us of a chicken offered us for sale when we were living in the hills in Jamaica. "The man wants a shilling for it, my sweet missis, but will take a sixpanse!"

But is it not what we all have to do in this world, more or less? Do we not begin life wanting not shillings, but great *doubloons*? And do not some of us learn to be content with our sixpence, and even to begin to fancy it is a lucky one after all?

We finally agreed upon three pounds a month, on condition that she would be willing to adapt herself to circumstances, and ready to exchange her projected position as nurse for that of housekeeper, if I did not succeed in getting another white servant to accompany us; and I dismissed her with the feeling that I had become possessed of an article likely to prove of invaluable service to me, but which would give me some trouble in controlling and subduing.

Succeeding events will determine whether this opinion was correct.

CHAPTER 2

Departure for the Transkei

Such was the nurse whom we now found awaiting our arrival at the docks, watching a group of Malays, whose gay attire looked bright and pleasant, and who would have made a more definite picture on my mind had it not been preoccupied by the bustle of going on board, and still more by the knowledge that in a few moments my invalid child would have to leave his faithful, loving Kitty, for the untried attendance of this hard individual, who was accompanied by a sister, even more hard-looking than herself.

But even iron can melt under warm influences; and I soon found both sisters in a melting mood at the prospect of parting. Poor Kitty, too, had been a perfect Niobe from the time we left Wynberg, and my own heart was rather heavy, though it did not indulge in the luxury of tears.

I flew to the cabin, made friends with the stewardess, and began trying to make things comfortable before Kitty left, as I felt sure baby would not take to his new nurse.

While engaged in this occupation, I was both touched and amused by Mrs. Gog's sister reappearing, and in pathetic accents imploring me to take care of her sister!—the said sister looking fully capable of taking care, not only of herself, but of our entire party into the bargain. However, I appreciated the feeling, and promised to do my best, little guessing how difficult it would be to keep my word.

The next day and a half were rather miserable, the south-easter continuing to blow so violently that we did not leave the dock until the afternoon of the following day. My baby, too, was almost frantic at losing his nurse, while, to increase my distress the ladies around would politely remark, "That child has got water on the brain,"

"If he were my child," &c. &c.

At last the battle was over, and the poor darling went submissively to Johanna Gog, who was quite flattered when he transferred his allegiance to her!

All this time we had "weather," and did not arrive at Port Elizabeth until the evening of the 9th, too late for passengers to go on shore. Next day there was a general exodus, and we now had the *European* almost to ourselves. We now settled down and brightened up a little, being fortunate enough to gain possession of an additional cabin.

We remained at Algoa Bay (Port Elizabeth), for five days, but did not care to go ashore, as the prospect from the ship was anything but tempting. We looked upon a dreary stretch of sand, backed towards the centre by something which seemed to have started in life with the intention of becoming a hill, but had collapsed in the effort, discouraged by the absence of trees or even bushes to support it.

In front of this low bank a town full of expensive-looking but painfully new and unhomelike houses had arranged themselves very tidily and respectably; here and there were churches and other buildings of a public nature, but no trees, no nothing, to relieve the eye or interest the mind.

To the right, a railway train looking like a toy, would suddenly appear and puff away conceitedly to apparently nowhere.—I thanked kind fate for not casting our lot here. Better far Kafir huts and mountain scenery than this sort of thing! However, I was told that the inhabitants were most energetic and prosperous; that beyond the barrier of sand they had actually made a green park or garden, for which the very earth employed, had to be brought from a distance; and I gave them my good wishes, though thankful not to be compelled to share the task.

Only one thing occurred to me, as I recalled the lovely harbours of the West Indies, the gorgeous tints, splendid scenery, and luxuriant vegetation of the Tropics—is it absolutely necessary that man should spend so much money and toil upon ugly places, while at a fraction of expense and fatigue he could convert the loveliest spots on earth into paradises almost fit for fairies to live in? Will no one say a kind word for the Tropics?

CHAPTER 3

Port Alfred

Though we did not admire Algoa Bay, we spent a very pleasant time there; and should not have murmured had our stay been even longer. The only passengers besides ourselves were two ladies, on their way to mission stations in the Transkei. One was a bonnie Highland lassie, whose demure demeanour and grave air were a quaint contrast to her glowing cheeks and bright eyes. I little guessed we should ever meet again, and still less under what tragical circumstances. It may have occurred to me that she might someday be my guest, but I little dreamt how soon I should be a suppliant to her for shelter.

On the 14th July we left Port Elizabeth at 4 a.m., arriving at the Kowie (Port Alfred) at daybreak. I remember a chilly shore, with some trees and green grass; also a misty rain, through which I faintly perceived some houses; but altogether it was a dull day, and we were glad enough to hear the dear old screw at work again, and know we were really off.

This day was charmingly fresh and fair; and after finishing the small amount of packing I had to do, I enjoyed my Sunday morning admiring the coast, which for the first time began to look picturesque. As we neared East London my interest increased, as my husband had spent some time there, and he soon began to point out to me the principal features of the scene.

The Buffalo River here flows into the sea, and its beauty is greatly enhanced by the richly wooded banks (almost worthy of being called hills) which rise on either side. The town has also grown on either bank of the river: East London, the port and commercial portion, being on the south; while Panmure, which contains the private residences of the merchants, &c., lies on the north bank.

We spent some hours enjoying the calm, fresh beauty of the scene, which looked so good and pretty, like a nice little child with her Sunday dress on; and I think I made the most of my enjoyment, because I knew a dangerous "bar" separated us from the shore, which had to be crossed with invariable discomfort and occasional peril, so (reversing the nursery custom) I took the jam first, making up my mind to shut my eyes to the pill which was to follow! In the end, it was all jam! for, through a piece of good fortune and Captain Ker's courtesy, we accomplished our landing most comfortably, and the bit in the journey to Kafirland which I most dreaded proved one of the pleasantest and easiest things in the entire route.

The *European* had brought a new lifeboat from England, to be used at East London, and during the afternoon the people in charge of the old one came out to see their new pet, and on their return to the port they landed some second-class passengers from the *European*.

We expected to have to join this contingent, and were prepared to do so contentedly, as that alternative was far preferable to the dreaded surf-boats of which I had heard so much. But while looking a little anxiously at the crowd, Captain Ker most kindly proposed our remaining until the following morning, when we could make a comfortable cruise in the new lifeboat.

I need scarcely say we accepted this kind suggestion, and by seven o'clock on Monday morning I was pretending to eat the sandwiches our good old stewardess had thoughtfully prepared for us.

While saying goodbye to the old lady, who had quite won our hearts by her good temper, Mrs. Gog was taking leave of several stewards on her own account! She had flirted right and left the entire voyage, and exhibited the happiest talent for turning her flirtations to good account, and combining sentiment with substantial comfort in the most practical manner! She now went on deck with the children, and, by the time I arrived there, I was just in time to see her merry face laughing out of the basket (which also contained my two children), all over the side, and half-way down into the lifeboat.

I meant the children to have gone with me, and must confess to one thrill of terror while they were perched up in the air; but soon had the pleasure of seeing them scramble out into the boat, where kindly sailor-hands welcomed and stowed them away safely. My turn came next, after which my husband descended, and was soon arranging us all in our places, reserving seats for the two "missionary" ladies who were to accompany us.

I shall never forget their look of horror at the whole of this basket-trick performance, and remember spending the next few minutes in trying to overcome their confusion, by making them as comfortable as circumstances would permit. This accomplished, we bowed our *adieux* to kind Captain Ker, and after a charming half-hour on the water in the delicious morning air, were soon over the dreaded bar (which, behaved most politely to us), landed in the eastern provinces, and looking most eagerly at an eastern province town in a very rudimentary state of existence.

It is rather a task to convey any distinct picture of what East London then was, to European readers, for I have seen nothing in England or on the continent to which I could possibly compare it. My own feeling, as I looked about me on landing, was that I had now realized my idea of the sort of town that would spring up in the neighbourhood of gold-diggings.

At that time the houses were nearly all made of corrugated iron, and looked more like over-grown packing-cases than anything else. I could not trace any definite line of streets; and though the town did not look very tumble-down, it did decidedly look very tumble-up!

Little heaps of gravel, or something of that kind; confusion and chaos confronted us everywhere. Here we would meet a bullock-wagon on its way up-country; there a group of British officers chatting together. Perhaps the next object encountered would be some Africander dame, very much overdressed, and looking exactly like a fashion-plate painted in wrong colours! After which one's eyes would be refreshed by the delightful vision of an English lady (probably the wife of some officer), in simple, becoming morning attire, advancing to meet her husband at the garden-gate, to receive the precious packet letters from home!

While mentally photographing these various "arrangements," we arrived at Dowell's Hotel, where we found a comfortable breakfast awaiting us, which we much appreciated after our morning *al fresco*.

After breakfast Edward and I started for the shore—I suppose it could not be called a dock—the customs quay, in search of our luggage, which had to follow in the lovely surf-boats I have recently mentioned.

Here we found ourselves in the midst of a bustling scene, the most numerous actors in which were Kafirs, whom I now saw for the first time. They were employed in unloading the boats, and carrying off the cargo in different directions.

Edward now placed me on guard, while he collected our luggage, and I found my duties rather onerous. The Kafirs would keep seizing my most treasured possessions, and I had to look very fierce to protect them. A customs' officer now came to my assistance, and between us we managed to maintain my rights, until Edward came to tell me that no more luggage could be procured that day, so we might as well return to the hotel.

On our way, Edward caught sight of an immensely tall, red-haired, and gentle-looking individual in the uniform of a private in the frontier armed and mounted police (now called Cape Mounted Rifles), who, on recognizing Edward, saluted, and crossed the road for instructions.

In order to prevent mystification, I think it best to explain that my husband is a civil engineer in the Government service, and that his appointment (at that time) was that of Inspector of Roads for the Transkei—a large district about a hundred miles in length (to the south of Natal, from which it is only separated by a bit of No Man's Land), bounded on the south by the great Kei River, and on the north by the Umtata; and it is not for a moment to be confounded with the Transvaal, which is an inland territory many, many hundred miles away.

At the time my husband entered upon his duties, this Transkei district was in a most unsettled state, and as he was engaged in boundary work between hostile tribes, Government thought it expedient to provide him with an escort of mounted police.

The person now encountered was a member of this escort, who acted as orderly to Edward, and who had now come down from the frontier in charge of the bullock-wagon, in which we proposed to journey to Kafirland. I shall call him Magog, the name I could not resist applying to him when I saw his gigantic, but feeble-looking frame, leaning against one side of the door of our hotel, while Mrs. Gog, our nurse, supported herself against the opposite side, my pretty baby laughing in her arms. Gog and Magog, of course! Now we ought to get on famously!

CHAPTER 4

Invitations

Magog now came forward to deliver his despatches, two of which proved to be kind invitations, containing friendly offers of hospitality during our somewhat difficult journey upcountry.

One of these came from Commandant Bowker (of the Frontier Armed and Mounted Police), who is so renowned throughout the colony for his generous hospitality and distinguished services.

The other invitation was a most friendly one from Mr. Cumming, then resident magistrate at Idutywa Reserve (our destination in the Transkei), begging us to consider his house our home on our arrival, and to remain there until we had arranged the furniture of our own future home, and made everything comfortable for the children.

These invitations rendered a slight change of plan necessary. Magog had brought down the wagon to East London, as we originally intended to begin our gipsy-journey there. As, however, my husband wished to see Mr. Bowker, to make fresh arrangements about his escort, we were glad to alter the route, and get a chance of accomplishing some portion of the journey by rail. My husband, therefore, decided to send Magog off again with the wagon and our heavy luggage, under instructions to meet us at King William's Town, on the common adjoining the property of the good commandant.

This satisfactorily settled, the rest of the day was spent in rearranging the contents of our boxes in such a way as to admit of parting with much of our luggage without inconvenience, and in vain endeavours to convince Mrs. Gog that a certain musical-box, possessed by that lady, was not an indispensable necessary of our existence; and that, much as we appreciated the dulcet strains which proceeded from this pretty little portable piano, we actually intended to dispense with its services during the next three or four days.

This was the first, but by no means the last occasion, on which that exasperating little musical-box became an instrument of torture to us. It was always appearing in some form or other—emerging from bandboxes, tumbling out of baskets on to the poor children's toes, banging against the back of one's head when jolting into holes during our wagon-journey, and appearing to possess the most wonderful faculty for knowing when and where it was not wanted, and always contriving to appear at that particular moment.

We did our best to lose it; but its fair owner looked too well after its interests ever to give us even the chance of forgetting it; until we almost fancied her ulster must be a disguise, and that we had engaged the companionship, for six months, of the *fine lady upon a white horse*, who so provokingly insists upon having *music wherever she goes*.

However, Mrs. Gog proved a wise woman after all; for in our Kafir home we found the cheery little musical box a perfect treasure; and on rainy days the children and junior servants were often to be found gathered round good Mrs. Gog, who made her instrument perform for their gratification with great pride, evidently thinking my own piano-playing very inferior to her music, and taking all the credit of the melody to herself.

But I must not too far anticipate our future experiences, for I had not yet even seen the wagon, which, to me, formed the link and barrier in one, between civilization and my untried life beyond the frontier.

However, that evening my husband and I strolled out for a little fresh air; and on a piece of waste land, which had ceased to be country, and not yet begun to be town, we found the Government wagon, with the oxen feeding around.

I can hardly do justice to the mysterious feeling of interest with which I regarded this very prosaic equipage—to my English eyes so uncouth, so uncomfortable, so utterly unfit for little tender children to travel in. It seemed like a great elephant that had come to take me away to a rough future, which I dreaded unspeakably, and yet was resolved to face. Still, in the clear starlight, with the bracing air blowing cool and fresh about my face, I fancied it looked kindly upon me; and, refreshed and strengthened, I began already to face the monster more cheerfully, and even to think of it in a friendly light.

Next morning the "Monster" started early for King William's Town, under the charge of Magog; and after a hasty luncheon, the rest of our party followed in an omnibus which .came daily to convey passengers to the railway station.

This omnibus was a very airy equipage, seeming to consist of a roof, no sides, and—some wheels. It was cool and shady and fairly clean, and I was so glad to get out into the fresh air, that I was not disposed to quarrel with anything; though the absence of springs, the rapid motion and the very bad roads, full of holes and ruts, made our drive not too charming.

However, there was movement and change of scene, which always have an unspeakable attraction for me; and when we arrived at the banks of the Buffalo River, I was quite charmed with the scenery. Most delightful hills, just high enough to be enjoyable; glorious trees, rich vegetation, with bright sunshine and a clear sky to throw a golden glamour over the whole, formed a fairy-like picture which remains in my mind after the details have passed away; and the silver shimmer of the river still shines in my recollection as a sunny souvenir of that brilliant winter afternoon. Winter! with such sunshine, and such scenery, and such foliage! Yes; even then I was clad in velvet and fur, not one whit oppressive in the fresh invigorating breeze, and soon—as shades of evening darkened—should I be glad to add still warmer wraps to my already winter clothing, and wonder wistfully if a cheery English fire would greet our arrival.

And now we arrive at the pontoon which is to convey us across the river to Panmure, which rejoices in the possession of the railway station.

I had never before seen a pontoon, and was all eyes and ears for what was to come next. We now descended a steep bank, and then found ourselves, omnibus and all, upon a sort of flooring, with a rope on each side.

"Where is the pontoon? "I asked.

"You are on it at the present moment," replied my husband, and then the truth began to dawn upon me that we were indeed moving, though noiselessly, across the water!

The effect was most delicious, and it hushed every voice until we gained the opposite bank. [1]

It was very delightful, and I heartily wished the rest of our journey up-country could be accomplished in the same luxurious manner.

It was too nice to last long; and just as I had settled down to enjoy it comfortably, a rude shock scrambled us up the opposite bank, and a rapid drive through the ugly environs of a railway station soon deposited us safely at the door.

We took our places in the train, and were just expressing our gratification at having a carriage to ourselves, when a gentleman of unmistakeable military bearing, and looking the personification of luxurious bachelorhood, quietly opened the door and took possession of a seat by the window.

I gave one look at nurse, who was in convulsions at the predicament; shot a despairing glance at baby's bottle, and a very anxious one at my husband,—who reassured me by looking quite happy.

We had hardly started before the new arrival made some courteous remark, to which my husband replied by addressing

---

1. If any lady readers should wish for a further description of a pontoon, I refer them to their friends in the Royal Engineers, who will doubtless be happy to tell them all about it. I do not feel equal to the task myself, as I belong to the dark ages before school boards existed, and merely attempt to describe what I saw, as it appeared to me.

him as Captain Grant, and I soon found they were not altogether strangers.

A year after, on my journey down again; I had the pleasure of meeting the very charming wife of Captain Grant, and of being introduced by her to their handsome circle of olive branches. I confided to her my terror of the supposed bachelor, and we had a ladies' laugh over my very great mistake.

After our new acquaintance had been presented to me, I was glad to give myself up to quiet enjoyment of the scenery, undisturbed by the long Transkei talk into which Captain Grant and my husband had drifted, and which chiefly concerned topics of which I knew nothing.

I was very tired, and the luxurious comfort and cleanliness of the well-cushioned railway carriage (at that time quite new), were most thoroughly appreciated in my quiet corner. The murmur of the gentlemen's voices was rapidly lulling me into dreamy forgetfulness of everything around, when a most gorgeously illuminated picture of richly-wooded mountain scenery arrested my attention, and effectually banished all wish for sleep.

"What is this? Where are we?" I demanded of my husband, who, knowing my love and admiration for beautiful hills and foliage, had reserved this as a pleasant surprise, in order to heighten the effect.

From this time until we reached Blaney, the journey was one long enjoy (if I may be allowed to coin a word), and I revelled in a perfect panorama of lovely pictures, each seeming more beautiful than the last, until the gem of all—the enchanting peep of the Nahoun—left me almost sated with loveliness, and willing to isolate (and thereby preserve) the remembrance of all this ethereal enchantment, by turning to other attractions and charms of our route.

Not the least of these consisted in the fact that my husband was interested in every inch of ground along the line. (I am going to talk "shop," so skip, fair readers, a little further on.) As I think I mentioned before, my husband had been detained for a short time the previous year at East London, as Government did not think it advisable to make surveys beyond the frontier just then, and while pending permission to proceed, he had been temporarily engaged in connexion with the railway.

He had received much kindness from his brother engineers, of whom he spoke quite affectionately; and now almost every station, curve and gradient, recalled some agreeable or amusing incident, and of course every episode had its special interest for me. I was also charmed with the comfort of everything; the carriages were not only furnished with springs, but were also provided with India-rubber blocks, and the easy swing was de-lightful.

CHAPTER 5

Kafir Huts and Kafir Kraals

We soon arrived at a most charming little station called Fort Jackson, where we had a nice interval for refreshment.

There was no fort, apparently, and—no Jackson!—not even a stone-wall!

(Please do not hold me responsible for this very bad joke. I am writing under the influence of the delicious cup of tea I enjoyed there, and mean no disrespect for America; a country in which I have all my life taken the deepest interest, and which I hope someday to see.)

Neither do I wish to convey the smallest reflection upon Fort Jackson. The refreshment-stall was deliciously clean and well supplied, and I only wish one ever had a chance of getting at an English country station as tempting a cup of tea as I enjoyed here in the wilds of Kaffraria.

But on leaving the little station all thought of creature-comforts was suspended, in the eager curiosity with which I was now reconnoitring the country, for the first glimpse of Kafir huts and Kafir *kraals*!

I daresay I might have seen them before; but during the earlier stage of the journey my whole attention had been so absorbed by the grander features of the scenery that I had not time for details as we whirled rapidly along. Besides, the mud huts and dusky people, in their brown blankets, are most difficult to discern in a general survey, as they harmonize wonderfully with the hue of the undulating grassland, and even a practised eye

30

may easily fail to perceive them.

Troops accustomed to foes arrayed in all the brilliant colouring of European uniforms may well be puzzled at first by the weird warriors who spring from an apparently unoccupied ground, and whose silent and stealthy steps would tax the ear of a Red Indian to hear.

At last my patience was rewarded by the appearance of several beehive-shaped mud huts, arranged in a circle; within hailing distance of another *kraal* (village) of a similar nature, which surmounted the crest of a neighbouring hill.

"You don't mean to say human beings really live in those fearful-looking things?" I exclaimed.

"Yes, indeed," returned my husband, "and very comfortably too! They have a fire made in the centre of the floor, in a depression of the ground, and are all as smoky and happy as possible. At night they curl themselves up in their blankets with their toes towards the fire, and if a baby or two happen to roll in and get burnt, it does not seriously affect their equanimity."

"Ah, I see you are an old traveller," I laughed; "but you shall inflict no more horrors upon me." And from that time I kept my first impressions to myself, and—thought the more.

What should I have said, had any one told me that before a year had passed I should spend sixteen weeks under shelter so scanty, so inadequate as protection against the elements; that I should look forward to the completion of a Kafir hut as a residence, with as much eagerness as was ever displayed by a cotton lord engaged in the absorbing interest of building a magnificent mansion for posterity!

Happily, I did not know what was in store for us, and enjoyed my first view of Kafirland with all the zest of one new to the scene.

"Now for the Kafirs!" I thought, and a few moments after my curiosity was gratified by the sight of some strange, sad figures, looking exactly as if they were dressed in terracotta, and apparently made of the same material; sharply defined against a background of white tents.

At first sight It was difficult to realize they were beings of the same nature with ourselves, endowed with immortality and capable of infinite development into good; but a second thought reminded me that we are all only clay after all, and that I was simply looking at red clay instead of white.

A third inspection also showed me that they were not so repulsive-looking as I had expected. I had been told that their clothing entirely consisted of red blankets, and that they also daubed their faces with red paint.

I had taken for granted that the red would be scarlet and their own complexions vermilion. In fact, I had conjured up a vague vision of a legion of Mephistopheles!!

I don't mean the nice Mephistopheles one sees on the stage, but that dreadful old thing with horns and a tail, which used to terrify and yet fascinate me as a child, in a Queen Anne's Prayer Book at home.

This red was brownish-looking, and of a rather agreeable tone, which harmonized well with the surrounding scenery, and gave them an unmistakeable air of being *Sons of the Soil*.

And now the Kafir group melts away, and I am looking at some quaintly dressed German settlers who crowd into the carriage. The lamps were lighted, and the children began to fidget and fret as bedtime approached; I must turn my thoughts from nature outside the carriage, to tiny, but tyrannous, human nature within; and I am not sorry when we arrive at King William's Town.

We now found to our dismay, that no carriage of any kind whatever was to be hired, either at the station or in the town; and that we must depend entirely upon our own resources to convey ourselves and our possessions to Commandant Bowker's house, which was ever so far away—quite the other side of the town.

I wonder how lame people manage. Do they never go out?

Chapter 6

Mrs. Gog Comes to the Rescue

Mrs. Gog now came to the rescue; coolly collared a couple of small boys, and insisted upon their conveying our goods and chattels, ourselves and "bairnies," to the residence of the commandant. We surrendered without discretion, for this self-constituted leader of our little expedition soon distinguished herself by losing her way and getting us all into difficulties. So, thinking we had had quite enough for the present of petticoat government, I ventured to suggest that my husband was perfectly qualified to take the reins; and under his guidance we proceeded slowly but surely to our destination, Mrs. Gog bringing up the rear; silent, but not subdued.

My husband was soon obliged to carry our elder child, poor little Henry, who tried hard to walk like a man, and stumbled sleepily along until his tired little toes tripped him up, when he reluctantly consented to be carried like baby, on condition he should be put down before we got to the house, and walk into the garden by the side of Mamma.

Under these circumstances we all found abundant occupation, and could not look about much, or form any but the faintest idea of the town.

We seemed to be walking along the middle of immensely wide roads, so wide at times that we could hardly distinguish the houses on either side; then crossing bits of rough ground, or passing through narrower streets bordered by small, shabby cottages; seeing a few quiet sort of people occasionally, but not noticed by them in any way. Sometimes one would recognize the uniform of a private in the F.A.M.P. (I can't afford to write Frontier Armed and Mounted Police every time, it uses too much ink); but there was little to arrest the eye, and a general atmosphere of dusty dullness seemed to pervade the whole. It seemed so strange to hear no carriages rolling along, and I had an indefinite impression that someone had died, and that we must not talk or make a noise.

This impression was deepened by my own sleepiness, the darkness of the night, and by the fact that we never seemed to get anywhere. At last, just as I had dozed off into a regular nightmare, and was expecting to spend the rest of my existence trudging along in this dreary manner, a hearty exclamation of pleasure from my husband cheered us all by the information that in a few more moments we should arrive at Mr. Bowker's door.

I was too tired to speak, but summoned up a nod and smile in return, crossed a little bit of grassland, and then, just as I felt I could not advance another yard, found myself passing through a gate, receiving a salute from several huge dogs, whose voices sounded cheerily through the gloom, and the kindest of welcomes from their master!

All this was in the leafy, lovely garden, perfumed by evening blossoms, and gladdened by Henry's merry, little voice. He had made friends already with the Kafir man-servant; and now a very neat handmaiden appeared, who carried off the children to some distant region, while I passed through the veranda and entered the drawing-room to be more formally introduced to our host.

I felt rather owl-like, emerging from the darkness into the pleasantly-lighted drawing- room, and too dusty to rest long in the cosy, easy chair covered by its spotless, snowy *kaross* (fur rug); so quickly flew to my chicks, to do all I could for them, and perform some very welcome and necessary ablutions before dinner.

On my return I caught sight of the soup-tureen shining in

the dim distance of a room beyond, and it was not long before the butler announced the agreeable fact, and we hungry travellers were enjoying its very acceptable contents.

We heard that our Jamaica acquaintance, Colonel Lanyon, had just left for Griqualand; that the Honourable Cecil Ashley had also just gone, and that the latter gentleman would probably precede us one stage ahead during the whole of our journey upcountry.

Both gentlemen had been guests of the commandant, who seemed always to have some visitor staying in the house.

I did not return to the drawing-room after dinner, as I had unpacking to do, and was glad to take my coffee into the children's room, and go early to rest.

To rest, but not to sleep! and after a night of fever I was favoured with an attack of ague in the morning, when I began to acquire my first impressions of that most puzzling, most provoking, and, above all others, most difficult to describe, climate of British Kaffraria.

Chapter 7

Trials and Tribulations of a "Grass-Widow"

The room I occupied had several French windows opening into the veranda, and through these I gazed admiringly upon a most gracefully arranged garden, flooded with brilliant morning sunshine.

Tropical fruits and flowers, gaily painted butterflies and birds, certainly do not look much like winter! and yet, at the same moment, my hands were aching through and through after the icy water in which they had been bathed; and blue with cold, and chilled to my very heart, I loaded myself with all the warm clothing I could find, and even then had to send for another shawl during breakfast.

The sunshine out of doors looked most inviting, and immediately after, I hastily put on a warm jacket, armed myself with a muff, and sallied forth.

For the first five minutes I was in ecstasies about the sunshine and the dry, bracing air; and did not grumble at the columns of dust which greeted us at every breeze, and which were rapidly converting my sable garments into raiment of orders grey. But after a mile or so of weary walking over dusty roads, I ventured to suggest that it was getting rather warm now.

"Warm!" rejoined my husband; "piping hot, you mean! Can't you take your jacket off?"

"What, here in the open street? "I demurred.

"Oh, yes; there is nobody looking."

So I thankfully take off the jacket which had felt so snug and comfortable only half an hour before.

The heat now rapidly increased, and by the time we arrived at Messrs. Irvine's stores, I was almost melting, and glad to rest while my husband attended to some Government business.

When this was despatched, Edward took me to look at some pretty Swedish furniture, which he thought particularly suitable for our little cottage in the Transkei, and I forgot the heat for a time in the interest of preparing for our future home.

This interest would have been considerably diminished, had I known that the greater portion of the things I was now selecting with so much care would only remain in our possession five short weeks; that the pretty china and glass would be smashed and desecrated by rough and savage hands; that the bedsteads would become the last resting-place of dying, wounded men; that many tables and chairs would be broken up for fuel; while the large stores of provisions we were now purchasing for our store-room, would be appropriated by the very men—no! I will not call them men—by the colonial gentlemen who should have been the first to protect me.

But the age of chivalry is past, and the fact of a woman happening to be for a time defenceless is no longer a claim to either sympathy or respect. *Au contraire*, the grass-widow is fair game—the target for every arrow—the unhappy butt of every sarcasm.

Women dislike her, because under the same circumstances, they would be fast; men distrust her, because she is not so.

Between Scylla and Charybdis, the poor little grass-widow becomes perplexed and bewildered. No one is 'perfect, and where every eye is on the watch to detect a flaw, it is not difficult to find fault. The more unsophisticated the nature, the more likely to fall before long into some little error of judgment, from which one true woman-friend might have saved her.

And then,—is not society severe to the poor, unconscious offender?

A hundred to one they unite in the noble, the courageous,

the dignified task of breaking the poor butterfly on a wheel, un-mindful that it may perchance prove a wheel of fortune, which will one day revolve and bear the little sufferer up again to the sunshine, while her persecutors are crushed into the dust.

CHAPTER 8

Shopping at King William's Town

My husband and I had contemplated remaining at Irvine's until the afternoon, so as to get through the greater part of our shopping; but at one p.m. the clerk modestly hinted that the establishment was about to be closed for an hour to enable the *employés* to get their dinners. We therefore left the store, and walked down what looked like the shoppiest street in the town, intending to make some purchases and return at the expiration of the hour. But, to our dismay, we found that all the shops were practically closed.

They were not literally shut up; but we found them all abandoned to the care of some especially elderly woman or particularly juvenile boy, and all hopes of eliciting any more eligible personage resulted in disappointment.

We went through the same dreary routine at every shop. After repeated appeals to the tender mercies of the concierge, he or she would open a door, through which we beheld a distant vision of a family party enjoying a most bountiful repast. Savoury smells issued from this sanctum, and the clatter of knives and steel forks clanged noisily in our ears.

A gruff rejoinder from the person wanted appeared to satisfy the concierge, who returned calmly to his normal occupation of catching flies on the window; and who from that moment became as stonily unconscious of our presence, as the Sphinx: of the pigmy tourists at her base.

We would then wait patiently (no, impatiently I mean) for

ten minutes or so, rapping with our umbrellas, coughing, and in other ways endeavouring to get somebody to take compassion upon us.

All in vain! and at last, in despair, we decided that as King William's Town was dining we must dine too.

(One would almost imagine there was some conspiracy between the restaurateurs of this place and the other establishments; for between one and two p.m. one is fairly driven into a pastrycook's!) Resolved to be fashionable or die; we strolled sadly on to B——'s Hotel, and I made up my mind to face the worst.

I knew pretty well what I had to go through.—East London had prepared me for that.

A hot, stuffy room; not one blind drawn down, and not one window drawn up! a Dutch trader on one side, my husband on the other; a missionary opposite, and at the head of the table a clerk from a store who will be on intimate terms with the family, and wear a red necktie while an atmosphere of onions and overcoats will pervade the whole!

However, it was not so bad after all.

As we entered the room every one rose politely, and the worthy host contrived to find time to usher me into my place, despite the manifold claims upon his time and attention which the duties of his position entailed upon him.

He was standing at a sideboard carving a superb sirloin; and my impression is, that a leg of mutton, some roast pork, and various other trifles, were also disappearing under the rapid touch of those skilful, surgical hands.

But this represented only a portion of his task—he had servants to scold, beverages to dispense, and, in addition, contrived to keep up an incessant stream of conversation with every individual in the room; evidently regarding his jokes in the light of an indispensable sauce.

The good man seemed quite distressed at my lack of appetite, and came kindly round to inquire, in tones of real concern, if there was nothing I could "fancy"?

I suggested a cup of coffee, hoping it would not give much trouble.

Trouble! on the contrary, a subdued murmur of approval went the round of the assembly, while mine host fairly beamed upon me.

Evidently, if there was one thing upon which B——'s especially prided itself, it was that balm of Gilead to a Dutchman—a cup of coffee!

True, I had frequently partaken of French coffee in France; the following year I should be regaled with Arabian *café noir* in a sultan's palace but these past and future pleasures were as nothing in comparison to the treat now in store.

I had yet to live; and in that magic beverage I should find the true and veritable *Elixir Vitæ*!

(It really was very nice, and I had the pleasure of praising it, in words that were not only kindly intended but strictly true.)

We now returned to our shopping like giants refreshed.—By this time everyone else seemed awake again; and the contrast presented by the bright and busy appearance of the town was so great in comparison to its apathetic condition an hour before, that one could hardly help fancying some magician's wand had been at work in the interim.

It was quite a transformation, and one almost expected to find some fairy columbine floating along to give a touch of grace to the picture, or, at the very least, to encounter half a dozen clowns to add a spark of animation to the scene.

But I fear Grace and Wit are lady-travellers who have not yet visited South Africa; and perhaps this is as well, for the soft wings of the one, and the delicate shafts of the other, would most assuredly become injured and blunted, from contact with the rough experiences which would everywhere surround them, while their sensitive natures would often quiver in anguish from wounds unconsciously, but ever constantly, inflicted.

Chapter 9

Farewell to Civilisation

This afternoon however, all went well; and the most artistic purchaser would have had no reasonable cause to complain of the pretty china, glass, &c.; from which I had the feminine pleasure of selecting the newest-oldest-looking, for our little cabin across the Kei.

The next three days were spent in "one continuous round of shopping," until I began to imagine myself metamorphosed into the far-famed Miss Flora McFlimsey of Madison Square, and to think my husband must be her friend Mrs. Harris! No, that long-suffering man must be rather Patience on a Monument in disguise; for a mortal Mrs. Harris might have put up with the shopping, but would most certainly have murmured at the weary walk which preceded and followed it, and which I only accomplished by reminding myself every five minutes of the delicious cup of tea which the kind commandant invariably had ready for me on my arrival in the veranda.

I should not have felt the fatigue so much had I not been suffering from ague; which clung to me in the most affectionate and exasperating manner the whole time we were at King William's Town. This was doubtless owing to the perpetual and violent changes of temperature; in the morning it was too cold to do anything; in the middle of the day it was too hot to do anything; and by the evening it was so cold again, that one might as well wait until the next day to do anything! (I am not responsible for this remark, which was the suggestion of a friend.) Poor old England! people call your climate changeable; what would they say to that of British Kaffraria! You are a respectable old lady, and content to wear a winter or summer dress for several months in succession; but this Africander damsel must don both on the same day, and wish for the other the whole time!

However, Sunday came at last, and nature attired herself in her fairest and most attractive dress, to do honour to the day of rest.

We did not go to church, as it was ever so far away; but I think church came to us, in the restful, peaceful calm which pervaded the whole place.

I also enjoyed a cosy time with my children again, for during the past week I had only had occasional peeps at them, and it was a perfect luxury to take dear baby on my lap again.

After breakfast we adjourned to the veranda, and feasted our weary eyes upon the lovely foliage and flowers in the garden below.

This garden pleased me very much—it was so gracefully untidy.

Someone said, "it would drive a Frenchman mad"; but my private opinion is, that the Frenchman would have taken possession of the most comfortable Madeira chair, lighted a cigarette, and made himself very happy!

I did not light a cigarette, but I did seize upon the most luxurious, low chair, and amused myself watching little Henry, who was vainly endeavouring to catch the brilliant butterflies which flew about in all directions.

The whole thing was quite a picture! Opposite to the veranda was a pretty, miniature lake, from the centre of which rose a tiny fountain, whose sparkling spray scattered silvery dewdrops upon the tall papyrus plants around, and then descended in graceful cadence upon the lilies which lay lovingly upon the water beneath.

Doves came to drink at this fountain, undisturbed by the presence of my fair-haired little boy; who chased the pretty butterflies fluttering about him, his white *puggaree* streaming in the breeze.

Beyond the little lake, one looked along vague *vistas* of trees laden with tropical fruit, brilliant foliage, and gorgeous flowers; all arranged so gracefully that a sort of enchantment seemed to pervade the whole.

Perhaps this charm was not lessened by the knowledge that on the morrow we were to bid adieu to civilisation, and commence our march towards the wilderness; and I felt as the explorer feels, when he bids farewell to home!

The whole of that peaceful Sunday will ever remain on my mind as an oasis of rest and serenity; framed by the circle of stormy events which preceded and followed it, and tinted *en couleurs de rose.*

I went to bed that night quite prepared to start early next morning; braced for any discomforts; rather wishing for a few hardships, and wondering what adventures would befall us before the journey was over!

CHAPTER 10

Ups and downs of a Wagon Journey

It was rather a bathos; when after being roused at some un-earthly hour, and having valiantly faced the icy cold water; trembling with cold and dying for the early coffee, I was informed by my husband that there was no chance of our starting that day, as the oxen had all been lost during the night!

Of course the day passed away, but it was very stupid—everything packed up, and a restless feeling prevented one's enjoying the many comforts about one.

It was quite a relief when, just before sunset, I heard a bright, cheery voice talking pleasantly to my little boy. My husband caught sight of me, and introduced the owner of the kindly voice as Captain (now Major) Robinson, Royal Artillery.

We had quite a merry little dinner, our new friend doing his best to invent or recollect every horrible story he could hunt up to prepare me for the future!

After dinner I went to my room, determined to remain there until I heard the oxen were really forthcoming; doing my best to put a brave face on our future, but inwardly quaking in the most craven, possible way.

However, next morning dawned brightly, and ushered in an almost tropical day, which I, with my love of sunshine, greatly appreciated, and which seemed to put new life and energy into us all.

It was Tuesday, the 24th July, 1877—a date which I may be permitted to chronicle, as it was the first step in a new career.

My husband did the work of seven men in futile attempts to start early; our Kafir drivers silently but stubbornly baffled all his efforts, and it was quite 11 a.m. before we fairly started.

The government wagon was drawn up in front of the gate, and two other wagons, which were to convey our furniture, &c., stood immediately behind.

I felt like Jacob going down into Egypt at the sight of this antediluvian array, and made up my mind not to express surprise if Noah's Ark appeared by way of a ferryboat when we arrived at the Kei.

Everyone knows by this time what South African wagons are like, so I will merely describe the interior arrangement, which my husband had superintended himself. Right across the wagon was fixed a sort of framework made of leather (called a *cartel*), on which were placed mattresses and pillows. On this we were expected to recline, and I found nurse and the children perched up quite comfortably. I, however, indignantly declined the idea of travelling in this lazy sort of fashion.

"No, indeed! I am going to sit up and look at the scenery. Do you think I am going through South Africa with my eyes shut?"

The kind commandant and Captain Robinson did all they could to prove to me the vanity of such a resolution, but of course I had my own way, and soon discovered I had made a mistake.

I started in grand style, and was just thinking how comfortable I was, when bump, dump, went the wagon into a deep hole! As for me, I was thrown violently on to my face in fall view of the gentlemen at the gate, whose kind advice I now tried in vain to take!

But I had lost my chance; and now, with the wagon in motion, it was simply impossible to accomplish what would have been perfectly feasible a few minutes before.

We were mounting the circle of hills by which King William's Town is surrounded; my husband had not yet arrived, and I did not venture to order the wagon to be stopped during the ascent, so I passed the first half-hour in great discomfort, and arrived at the summit, a sadder but a wiser woman. I now looked down upon King William's Town, which lay at the bottom of a green basin like an egg that was going to be beaten. I wished some colossal cook would take compassion upon it and shake it up a little! It seemed strange that the first settlers should have pitched their tents down in a hole, when they might have perched like eagles, upon those charming hills.

I now no longer marvelled at the close atmosphere which had suffocated me at midday, nor at the ague I had suffered from morning and evening.

I am not learned in military matters, but could not help also thinking King William's Town but ill adapted for defence. Surely thousands of Kafirs could easily and simultaneously surmount this circle of hills, and then would not the town be almost at their mercy? If I were the good Genius of the place, I would build a few martello towers on the summit of those hills, and station a guard to give notice of an enemy's approach.

But here come—not the enemy—but two horsemen, who soon resolve themselves into my husband and his orderly.

Their arrival brightened us up considerably, and Edward halted the wagon to pack me up comfortably before proceeding any farther.

I felt this was more than I deserved, after my obstinate little fit of conceit, and resolved to be a model of meekness for the future!

As usual, the Valley of Humiliation soon became sweet and pleasant, and we jogged along pretty comfortably for about two hours.

The awning had long since been drawn down to protect us from the heat. Baby had for some time been asleep; and, lulled by the dull thud, thud, of the wagon, I was rapidly imitating his example, when a voice shouted in my ear, "Here we are! "I patiently submitted to be unpacked like a sort of bundle, and deposited on the grass, where, to my astonishment, I instantly collapsed.

The journey had. been so comparatively easy that I was surprised to find myself trembling all over, every limb cramped, and a most uncomfortable sensation of having been pounded in a mortar, and afterwards shaken in a sieve, "pervading one's entire being" (as our cousins across the Atlantic would say).

Feeling all attempt at dignity would be an utter failure, I meekly followed n

urse and the children into a funny little house, known as "Gunn's," where a cheerful-looking woman received us pleasantly, and inquired if we wished to be shown into a dressing-room.

I replied in the affirmative, and now another shock awaited me.

After my experiences outside the house I ventured rather timidly to the looking-glass; but modestly as I prepared for the "first view," I must confess that I received a disagreeable surprise!

What had become of the carefully-arranged plaits upon which I had expended so much patience in the morning?

A dusty wig, resembling an old mop more than anything else, bristling with pins apparently bent upon flying to every point of the compass at once, confronted my bewildered gaze. A face begrimed with dust, and collar to match, completed my discomfiture; and a glance at my dust-laden hat and clothing, put the finishing stroke to my mortification.

"Well," I thought, "Venus herself could not hope to look even respectable under such circumstances, so I must not murmur;" and armed with a bagful of brushes, sponges, and towels, I turned away to battle with the dust.

Most welcome ablutions followed, and by the time my husband came to summon me to lunch, I felt a little more like a "Member of Society."

We found the repast spread in a tidy little dining-room delicious bread and butter; some cold mutton and chutney, and preserves; the whole flanked by a coffee-pot and very clean cups and saucers. The steel forks were rather a trial at first, especially as mine insisted upon constantly stabbing me; however, I soon became more expert, and, by the time I had poured out the coffee, began to feel quite at home.

The "gude wife" waited upon us, and on our departure actually ran after the wagon with an offering of some of her delicious butter by way of a parting gift.

"Do take it, mum! don't be vexed! you will get nothing so good where you're agoing to."

I accepted it most gratefully, and the good creature stood smiling and nodding at the children until we were out of sight. We continued our journey along grassy, undulating, but not specially interesting country, until about 4 p.m.; when a change crept over the atmosphere, and a chilly breeze (feeling trebly cold after the tropical sunshine of the previous hours) compelled us to halt and prepare for the evening journey. My husband rode up, and, giving his horse to the orderly, made us all get out and wrap ourselves in all the shawls we could muster. Meanwhile a beautiful white *kaross* was laid upon the mattress, and we were put back into the wagon like so many dolls. My husband then tucked us up inside the *kaross* and departed, imagining we were comfortable! !

Had I only had to share the *kaross* with my children, we should have been cosy enough, but unfortunately it had also to shelter our nurse, poor Johanna Gog!

This was not very agreeable, and became still less so day by day, as that worthy woman's dress became more thoroughly permeated with dust; especially as I discovered that she did not recognize the necessity of ablutions *en voyage*.

"What is the good of washing when you are going to be black again in half an hour?" she would exclaim in reply to my gentle hints that her personal comfort would be increased by a nightly tub.

I did not dare to say much for fear of losing my "treasure," and felt grateful that, for appearance' sake, she did try to keep her face and hands clean!

But though I suffered silently, I did suffer; comforting myself however with the reflection, that the journey would not last for ver.

The wagon now steadily jogged along until we arrived at a place known at that prehistoric period as "Hangman's Bush," but which now rejoices in the almost equally ugly, and far more inappropriate name of "Kei Road."

It was now about eight o'clock in the evening, and I was not sorry to learn we were to rest here for the night. I had plied the children steadily with biscuits and milk all the afternoon, and they had done pretty well; but though I had tried to munch a biscuit or two, it had been a failure, as I was too thirsty to eat.

What would I not have given for a cup of afternoon tea! but that luxury was unattainable on this occasion, as my husband could not "out-span," as we had lost so much time in the morning.

For about two hours I had been telling stories to Henry; these were succeeded by hymns; and finally the little man fell asleep in a futile attempt to say his prayers.

I was now glad to rest myself, and rather enjoyed lying there looking up at the golden stars.

My husband rode up for a few kind words now and then, and when about half an hour's distance from our destination, directed the orderly to gallop on and secure rooms for us at the hotel.

I also put in a plea for plenty of hot water, as I wished to send the poor chicks clean to bed, as we should not have time for much bathing in the morning.

Our kind pioneer did his work well, and by the time we arrived everything was ready, and in a few minutes both little ones were luxuriating in one big tub.

Chapter 11

A Romance in Real Life

After seeing the children comfortably into bed, I went to look for my husband; who at once took me into a good-sized dining-room. Here a long table was laid, almost luxuriously, for "high tea," and I was surprised to find everything so comfortable. Bright plate, glass and china, glistened and glittered upon a most immaculate tablecloth; tea and coffee were being served; some hot *entrees* only awaited my arrival to be handed round; and several varieties of cold meat, cakes, and preserves, made a picture of substantial comfort which we felt by no means inclined to severely criticize after our long journey.

Besides all these good things there were fresh eggs, butter, and—that indispensable adjunct to every Dutchman's meal cheese at hand; so I think a word of compliment is really due to our host, good Mr. Heath.

"We shared this entertainment with a motley group of travellers, and I was the only lady present; but I had nothing to complain of. All behaved in the most courteous way, and there was nothing to distress me except the feeling that I was a painful constraint upon them, and that they must be longing for me to depart.

The worst of it was they all seemed too shy to eat, and I made up my mind not to come in to breakfast until they had all had a good start.

Having made this resolution, I summoned courage to look

about me, and found to my astonishment that the entire wall-surface of the room was covered with oil-paintings.

My interest was increased when I was told a romantic story in connexion with them. It seems they were the work of a young artist, who, in despair at the death of his bride, had tried to alleviate his sorrow by the vicissitudes of a wandering life.

The scenes depicted were chiefly continental, and reminded me of a dear, old drawing-room in Cheshire, which had been decorated by the great Stanfield in his early days: they recalled the grand piano, and the quaint garden beyond the great window, and I almost fancied I was a girl again, playing dreamy cadences with flowers as my only audience; gazing lovingly at the beautiful scenes by which I was surrounded, and wondering wistfully whether I should ever have the happiness of seeing them in reality! With an effort I roused myself to face the answer to these girlish questionings.—Yes, my longing for a Crusoe life had been gratified, and though South African scenery had been a little disappointing, lovely Jamaica had not; and I felt grateful that I had been privileged to behold her tropical beauty. But now, all I had to look forward to was a monotonous existence in the desolate Transkei; and, saddened somewhat by the thought of the stagnation which awaited me, I bethought myself of my duties, and finding nurse had thoughtfully performed them all for me, departed to bed to prepare for the march tomorrow. The children, nurse, and I, shared a most comfortable room, and were soon all sleeping soundly after our long and fatiguing journey.

Chapter 12

Picnic in the Prairie

My husband slept in the wagon; "on guard," as he called it, and his orderly was also on duty, but I fear the "Guards "would both have run some risk of being summoned before a court-martial, had there been any authorities to call their conduct into question, for their presence did not prevent the commission of a most daring theft.

Next morning, just as we were all ready to make an early start, my husband discovered that some indispensable part of the harness had disappeared, and this occasioned a delay of about two hours.

However, we did get off at last, after an interval of waiting which I beguiled by a complimentary chat with, our landlord, who had served in the West Indies and seemed pleased to talk about Jamaica.

Before leaving, we procured provisions for a midday meal, as we were to picnic in the wilderness. I rather liked this idea, and as the weather was simply charming, the morning's "trek "was really not disagreeable.

About 3 p.m. we halted, on the bank of a river called the Gnubie (pronounced Ganúbie), and, our oxen having been out-spanned, prepared for our picnic in the prairie.

I ought to have mentioned that our party had been rein-forced by the arrival of three more of my husband's escort, so I felt well protected, with no less than five cavaliers in attendance. (What there was to protect me from, I don't quite know, unless it was—snakes!) However, I did not feel disposed to question the necessity, or doubt the valour, of the four gentlemen, who acquitted them- selves as most capable knights of the kettle, making a fire and cooking our dinner in less than no time.

I don't think they had the least faith in a housekeeper under six feet high, for they would not even allow my maid to "lay the table." However, we did not mind this ignominious treatment, and were all very happy; the children enjoying the fresh air and the flowers, and little Henry as glad as we were to move about and exercise his cramped limbs a little.

When summoned to dinner, I need hardly say we admired and appreciated everything, and not for worlds would I have ventured to suggest that the tea, meat, and even butter, were all flavoured by the tin plates and cups in which they were served.

Nurse and I, however, registered a private vow to take the commissariat into our own hands for the future, and never to travel again without a small supply of common china (packed among glass-towels, with which to wipe it afterwards).

In justice to my sex, I must also add that we had suggested this arrangement, but were silenced by the reply that everything was all right, and that during our journey we were to trust entirely to the superior wisdom and forethought of Man.

After that, we could but submit, and determine to reserve a sweet revenge for the next wagon journey, when of course we intended everything should be done in perfect style!

When our picnic-dinner was over, I took care of the children, while nurse washed clothes for baby in the river, drying them afterwards on the *veldt*.

We had plenty of time, making a lengthy halt, our oxen not being in good condition.

We also took advantage of this opportunity to wash our hands and faces in the river, and were quite refreshed when our "Commandant" gave the order to start again.

Now came a difficult little bit. The wagon had to cross the river, which was full of large, rocky stones, which I preferred stepping across, to being jolted over them in the wagon. My husband preceded me, carrying little Henry in his arms, and I intended nurse and baby to cross in the same manner. My dismay can therefore be imagined when I found the wagon—nurse and baby and all—was already half across the stream, but was reassured by nurse's merry laugh, and heard afterwards both had rather enjoyed the fun; baby sleeping comfortably, and nurse's vigorous frame apparently none the worse for the jolting it had received.

After the exertion of jumping from one stone to another, I would fain have cried for mercy, but was immediately compelled to climb a steep hill, and could not get into the wagon again until we had arrived at the summit.

From that time the journey was all an ascent, as we had to rise about 2000 feet, and the beautiful scenery really did compensate me for the knocks and bruises I received while sitting up to admire it.

It was not all disagreeable either; sometimes after a particularly unpleasant shaking, being hurled alternately from one side to the other, one would gain the summit of a hill and go on quite peacefully for a mile or so.

Then it was delicious; one reclined upon the nicely-arranged cushions and gazed without fatigue at the lovely, ever-changing panorama of hills and valleys which one enjoyed all the more after the hard times.

Our dear little son was also having a pleasant change by riding on horseback the greater part of the afternoon. He was then in splendid nerve and very good health, and the brave little man sat up splendidly in front of his father, and was not in the least alarmed even when galloping quite fast.

When papa was tired, the gentlemen of our escort kindly took the child upon their horses; and by sunset, when cold drove him reluctantly back to the wagon, he was so comfortably fatigued that he fell asleep almost immediately, and did not awake even on our arrival at Dry-bush. (*Dreie-bosch* perhaps I ought to spell it.) The hotel here was burnt to the ground a few weeks afterwards during the war; and in the destruction of the house, also perished some wall-paintings, by the artist who had decorated Heath's place at Hangman's Bush.

CHAPTER 13

The Empress of Delhi

We went through a similar routine to that of the evening before, but were fortunate in losing nothing during the night; and should have made an early start had not a regular old-fashioned Scotch mist delayed us.

This old friend (or rather old foe), gave us a "damp, unpleasant" reception, and reminded us pretty sharply (old friends being privileged to tell one home-truths), that we were nearly 3000 feet above the sea.

We might just as well have been down a coal-mine, or in the Thames Tunnel, for aught we could see of the landscape!

Everything was covered by a cloud, and looked as if Dame Nature was having a big washing-day.

The mist detained us until nearly eleven o'clock; and just as we were starting, who should appear but our friend Captain Robinson, who rode up for a moment to inquire, "Well, Mrs. Prichard; how do you like South African travelling now?"

"Very much; not half so bad as I expected," I laughed.

Whereat he shrugged his shoulders: "Glad you like it;"—and rode away to prepare his servants for our arrival at Komgha, as he had kindly invited us to rest that night at his house.

The morning passed slowly, as the scenery was uninteresting; flat, and with hardly a tree or bush to relieve the monotony.

We were on a high table-land which stretched away for miles of dreary dullness, and I was struck by the almost death-like appearance of the scene.

It was rather cold too, and on these raw, chilly days, the Kafirs remain as much in their huts as possible, and you may travel many miles without meeting a single creature.

Still, I rather liked the monotony for once, as the road was comparatively smooth and even, and I enjoyed a quiet rest, after the ups and downs of the previous journey.

About two o'clock in the afternoon the sun began to shine more brightly; and almost at the same time the scene changed. Wagons and horsemen passed us on the road; groups of Kafirs were to be seen (some in semi-European costume), and in a few moments we arrived at the rising, little, frontier-town of Komgha. The inhabitants wisely retain the characteristic name, instead of calling it West London, or something else equally absurd.

I could hardly look about much, for I was hurriedly attempting to give a few civilizing touches to our disordered attire before we arrived at Captain Robinson's pretty little house; which was, I fear, somewhat desecrated by the group of sunburnt, dusty travellers; who however received a most kindly welcome from the hospitable owner, who was at the door to receive us, engaged in giving directions to his domestics to minister to our comfort in every possible way.

The said domestics rather interested me, both being importations. One was a *coolie* from India, and another a Creole from the Mauritius, with whom his master conversed in French.

All the servants were most obliging, and did their very, very best to carry out their master's directions. They gave us a charming little dinner; and I well remember how I enjoyed using the dainty old china, which was such a contrast to the tin cups and plates of the day before.

After dinner we did our duty by the town as new arrivals, by going out for a walk; but we could not find the streets, and the houses seemed so far away from each other that they did not look very neighbourly. However, Komgha was at that time in a very juvenile state of existence, and only wanted drilling; for when I revisited the place about fifteen months after, I found the town very much improved, and far more compact-looking than the year before.

Our shopping was tolerably satisfactory. We managed to procure some boots for poor little Henry, my husband insisting upon his being provided with the kind usually worn by children in the Transkei—dreadful brown things, with brass toes. It was a bit of a trial to encase his pretty feet in these clumsy-looking concerns; but I knew my husband was right, and had to submit to circumstances.

Had I known how soon our communication with the colony would be cut off, I should have made many more purchases; but as it was, our walk was soon over, and after unpacking and tidying the wagon, a game with, the children, coffee, and photographs, finished the day.

After sunset it became very cold, and I was glad of any excuse to go early to rest; feeling weary and anxious to be ready for the next day's journey, which would be a long one.

I now had a foretaste of some of our after-experiences, and slept or tried to sleep for the first time in my life, on the floor.

It seems our host was moving, or something of that sort, and had just sent away his larger furniture, bedsteads, &c. Fortunately there was one for the children and nurse, for which I was glad; but I was equally amused and charmed at the idea of sleeping on the floor—"like a real tin soldier," as my little boy said.

It was really very comfortable, and I should have slept well enough if I had not been too tired and feverish to appreciate the very warm *kaross* which covered me. The bed consisted of a small mattress, a pillow, and this handsome *kaross* (white fur rug), which was a sort of combination affair—sheets, blankets and *couvrette*, in one.

I could not sleep, but I was quite amused, and rested quietly, looking dreamily at the miscellaneous collection of curios, which made the room quite picturesque in the half- light.

If I had not a very feminine sort of couch to repose upon, I had at least a lady's equipage to wash with, for I had the honour of using a golden toilet-service which had been the property of the Empress of Delhi!! Who this lady was I know not; nor do I vouch for the truth of the story, which was communicated to me with, great ceremony by the *coolie* himself!

I can however, vouch for the beautiful Indian workmanship, which charmed me, though I confess to a plebeian preference for china or marble in things of this kind.

I became bewildered at last, looking with half closed eyes from the unwonted elevation (is it an elevation?) of the floor, and must have fallen asleep—for I was dreaming that the Empress of Delhi was scolding me fiercely for daring to desecrate her grand, gold service—when I became aware that candle-light had given place to cold, grey day-light, and that the infuriated Empress of my dreams was in reality the *coolie*-servant, who was knocking at the door with the information that my "master" (husband) had already taken his early coffee, and that I must drink mine quickly, as he wished to start before breakfast.

CHAPTER 14

Our first meal in the Transkei

We really did get off early today, though not without breakfast; and the air was keen and bracing when we started; but before long the sunshine warmed us so genially that we began to
lay aside our wraps, and by midday we were panting in a tropical
temperature, our winter clothing almost unbearable under that
blazing sun.

We were now descending into the valley of the Great Kei
River, that glorious boundary between Cape Colony and the
Transkei; and I felt a thrill of excitement almost amounting to
awe when I was informed that in a few more hours we should
cross the frontier.

A solemn silence reigned over the whole party—the suffo-
cating atmosphere depriving us of all energy—and the wagon
descended the steep gradients of the road almost as silently and
heavily as if we were all sinking into Avernus. The oxen looked
as sulky as possible, and the very drivers forbore to "yak!"—the
frightful noise they had kept up almost incessantly, by way of
stimulus to the pace of the oxen.

My husband and his escort sat their horses as silently as if
they were a funeral *cortége*, and I think I was the only member of
the party who had a spark of animation about me.

I can claim no credit for superior energy on this account; for
I was really interested in the scenery, and eager to seize every
picture before it was gone.

The rather narrow, and very rugged and rocky road, had apparently been cut out of the side of the mountain; as the hill rose high on one side, while a precipice yawned upon the other.

Tropical foliage adorned the mountain, and clothed the deep ravines with, beauty, and in the distance I beheld the blue mountains behind which lay our future home.

Little did I guess how soon we should have to leave that home, and still less did I dream that on the summit of one of those beautiful hills we should pitch our camp for months; while another point in the landscape would become sacred to me while life should last, as the earthly resting-place of the fair-haired darling whose beautiful eyes were now looking at me so lovingly—the brave little hero bearing so patiently the heat and fatigue, and never adding to our troubles by a single cry.

I was very glad for his sake when we arrived at the bank of the river, as we should shortly be able to obtain rest and refreshment. This was however, only to be procured on the other side, so we had to cross as well as we could.

Nurse and baby preferred remaining in the wagon, and jolted over without any accident, while my husband carried little Henry across, and I followed as fast as I could.

I am a perfect salamander,—have worn winter clothing while crossing the Line, and have never been heard to murmur at any amount of sunshine except on this occasion, when I must say, I toiled along, feeling as if I were being baked in an oven and scorched at a furnace at the same time. I could hardly drag myself across, and that dreary space which had to be traversed before gaining the opposite bank seemed simply interminable. I was too tired to care to look about me in that painful glare; but could I have done so the scene would not have been devoid of interest, especially to the wife of an engineer.

The great bridge over the river was then in course of construction, under the able direction of Mr. Newie, C.E., and at any other time I should have been much interested in the apparatus connected with the work, which lay about the bed of the river and surrounded us on every side. As it was, I had enough to do to avoid these obstacles and pick my way, sometimes over bridges consisting of a single plank, sometimes springing from rock to rock, and, finally, clambering up a very steep and sandy bank, which felt so hot that one could hardly walk over it.

A few minutes afterwards we arrived at the hotel kept by good Mrs. Hahn, and that worthy dame was giving us the brightest of welcomes.

I now stood, for the first time in my life, inside a Kafir hut, for at that time this was all the accommodation Mrs. Hahn had to offer.

It was very large and well-constructed, made of the usual basket-work and mud, and with a roof of thatch.

The ground-floor was divided into four compartments, lighted by single panes of glass let into the sides (about the size of the scuttles on board ship), but the rooms were rather dark, as the ceilings were very low.

Most of the sunshine came through the doors; one at each end of a narrow passage which divided the hut from east to west, which good arrangement ensured a certain amount of light and heat until the sun went down.

Every traveller will know that our one cry was "Water, water!" and I was indeed thankful to take the dear children into the room provided, and with nurse's assistance to give them a thorough washing. That accomplished, the poor little birds dipped their beaks into the glasses of nice milk brought them by our worthy landlady—a coloured woman married to a German.

My husband had often sung her praises to me, and we were better prepared to be very good friends.

She insisted upon my using her own toilet-vinegar to bathe my poor face, which was burnt and blistered almost beyond recognition; telling me, she "owed her own complexion entirely to its constant use."

Considering the good soul's beaming countenance was a few shades darker than a well-baked cottage loaf, and was thickly covered with a perfect forest of freckles, I am afraid this announcement did not produce the effect upon me which it was intended to create. However, I contrived to look happy, and felt really grateful for its cooling influence, and for the goodnature which made my kind hostess's *mulatto* face bright and pleasant to look upon, in spite of its colour and texture.

On looking round the room I found it was adorned in every direction with empty toilet-vinegar bottles, and I really think Monsieur Kimmel would have felt inclined to present the good woman with a five-pound note on the spot, for really she was quite an advertising medium.

Our *toilettes* completed, we now adjourned to the best parlour, to partake of a rough and ready kind of meal, for which our hostess made many apologies; our escort meanwhile getting something to eat in another room, as they would not hear of joining us, though I begged them repeatedly to do so. I hope they fared better than we did, for I cannot say the meal was very appetizing.

We had come at an unlucky moment; the bread was nearly black, and so intensely sour, that in spite of being very hungry, little Harry and I could not force it down. The meat had only been killed on our arrival, and was uneatable; nothing but ducks' eggs was forthcoming; and though I did try one of these, it was a failure, without decent bread and butter to take off the richness.

However, the tea and milk were simply delicious, and that made up for everything! I bethought me of our own stock of Huntley and Palmer's always tempting biscuits; procured them from the wagon, and so did very well.

The children dipped their biscuits into their milk, and mine went very well with my tea; while Edward ate everything with the appetite of a hunter, and I sat and wondered at him, until I remembered that he was more accustomed to frontier fare than I was.

So ended our first meal in the Transkei.

Beauties of Climate and Scenery

After we had finished our biscuit food and paid for all the things we had not eaten, we got into the wagon, and were glad to find that we were again to climb to higher ground. All through that pleasant afternoon we were passing through beautiful scenery, and greatly enjoyed the pure air of the highlands.

About an hour after sunset we arrived at Toleni, and as I dismounted from the wagon I beheld a most beautiful sight. A bushfire was raging upon the distant hills, and this always brilliant spectacle was on this occasion singularly vivid.

Two distinct lines of light stretched in unbroken regularity right across the horizon, and one could almost fancy it was a special illumination prepared for some welcome guest.

Of course we took the compliment to ourselves, and accepted it as a good omen for the future.

I might rather have imagined that it was an augury that the whole country would soon be in the flames of war; but fortunately I could not foresee the angry future, and went merrily into the house, resolved to consider this a welcome home.

We were at first told that the "wife was away," that "the servant had gone home;" and so many difficulties seemed to stand in the way of our remaining, that, too weary and faint to argue the matter, I was about to submit and suggest that we should sleep in the wagon and have some supper cooked at a camp fire, when Mrs. Gog (for the second time) came to the rescue.

I don't know what she did, for I was left in the dark with

the children, but I heard her bustling energetically hither and thither; talking English, Dutch, and Kafir, all at the same time, and rousing up the whole place with her life and energy.

She hunted up a Kafir woman, and soon the two were laying the table properly Mrs. Gog impressing upon the girl that her Missis was a lady of most delicate materials, and a personage entitled to receive the utmost consideration and respect.

In deference to my supposed exalted rank, the poor Kafir-woman flew about like one possessed, and soon a fairly comfortable meal was prepared in the dining-room, while a hot bath was steaming in the room beyond; Mrs. Gog taking care that snowy sheets and dainty pillowcases were provided for "her Missis and her children."

Tired out, we could not eat much, but we did appreciate the comfortable night's rest we all enjoyed, and felt quite fresh and eager for the day's adventures, when good Mrs. Gog appeared next morning with a hot cup of coffee, accompanied by the roughly given, but kindly meant admonition, to drink it up at once, "if I didn't want to rattle my teeth out of my head with ague, for really the morning was that cold, that she felt half froze herself." She further assured me that she had taken the whole *ménage* into her own hands; that a gorgeous breakfast was already being prepared; and that I should be treated like a lady "as long as her name was Johanna Gog."

There was no resisting this climax! I laughed so much that the snowy sheets ran a risk of imbibing the coffee intended for me; so I jumped up, whipped my good Johanna out of the room, and was thankful to begin my *toilette* with the hot water my "treasure "had thoughtfully brought for my use.

We made a substantial breakfast; and it was well we did so, as we had a lengthy "trek" in store, and the morning air was so fresh and bracing that had a second meal been in readiness, I verily believe we could have demolished it even one hour after starting.

I hope I shall never forget that hour! Is ever since, and never before, have I so fully realized the exquisite ecstasy of the mere fact of existence. The air seemed like crystal, and had a most exhilarating effect upon one. The sunshine was enchanting, neither too much nor too little; and the scenery was superb.

A hill rose before us, the lovely valley of the Kei was close at hand, and in the distance range upon range of glorious hills rolled grandly along the horizon; while the stately Amatola mountains seemed to close in and reign over the whole—kings and patriarchs in one.

Under such circumstances, who could remain in a close, stuffy wagon?—Not I, at all events.

I started up the hill, trying to walk sedately, as became a sober matron. But even walking was not sufficient exercise in such an atmosphere. I fairly danced with happiness , and soon my husband and I were racing up the hill, like a couple of children out for a holiday, while little Henry clapped his hands for joy, and nurse laughed in unison from the depths of her sun-bonnet.

(I must beg leave to state that our escort were all out of sight, having been sent off in different directions; one to the house of a missionary, to beg kind Mrs. Ross for some milk; another to Colonel Eustace, with a message of regret at being compelled to decline Mrs. Eustace's most kind invitation to visit them *en route;* a third to gallop to Ibéka, to ask Mrs. Barnett if she would be good enough to receive us for that night; and a fourth to prepare things at home as much as possible for our arrival.)

So we were quite *en famille*, until one of our cavaliers met us near Cunningham, with two bottles of milk for the children, and a bouquet of roses for myself, sent by good Mrs. Ross, to whom I was frequently afterwards indebted for many acts of considerate kindness.

CHAPTER 16

The Last Stage

We halted about midday at Butterworth, which looked more like a town than anything we had seen since leaving Komgha. [1]

We had a picnic on the *veldt*, just far enough from the houses to be out of the way. There was nothing interesting about the place. It seemed neither town nor country, and I was not sorry when we received orders to march.

We now traversed a very lonely piece of prairie, and I did begin to realize that we were in Kreli's country; in the very heart of Gcalekaland.

Occasionally we would pass Kafir *kraals*, and the lean, starved-looking dogs would rush out and bark at us; but I do not remember meeting a human creature for several hours, during which we did not even see a herd of cattle or a flock of sheep.

I was gazing earnestly at everything, straining my eyes for my first glimpse of Kafirs beyond the Frontier; and the utter silence and intense loneliness of the scene were beginning to exercise almost a soporific influence upon me; when, at a turn of the road, a trio of real Kafir belles suddenly appeared behind the wagon, "apparently starting out of the ground" (as Lord C. would say), and looking as much at home with us as if they had formed part of our retinue during the entire journey.

As I could not speak Kafir, I nodded, smiled, and kissed my hands to them, at which they laughed with delight like children, and apparently said something pleasant in reply.

1. Pronounced Koomka.

Feeling we had established something like amicable relations, I ventured to throw a biscuit to one of them, and was quite touched when I saw her divide it into three equal portions, and hand one of these to each of her sisters.

Finding they received my overtures so graciously, I amused myself throwing biscuits and pennies at them as long as I had any; little Henry assisting me, chattering away to the terracotta ladies as sociably as possible.

All this time they kept up with the wagon; advancing with a stately tread which never hurried, and yet got over the ground very rapidly.

The three walked in the most affectionate manner, with their arms entwined about each other, so that they really reminded one of the group of the Graces.

So far as beauty was concerned, few classical figures could have exceeded their grace. Their hands, feet, and ankles were all most delicately formed; and their oval faces, beautifully shaped heads, and glowing, glorious eyes; made one forget the thick noses and lips which prevented their being perfectly handsome according to our standard.

They really were good types, not only of the best-looking Kafir women, but also as specimens of native dress.

They were of course daubed with red ochre, and their dress consisted of a couple of small blankets, coloured to match their complexions.

One blanket formed the tunic, and another the shawl or *pallium*; the latter being clasped by an enormous brooch on one shoulder, and both garments hanging in rich folds about their graceful figures.

These blankets were further adorned with a perfect mass of embroidery, consisting of black braid and white buttons; arranged in geometrical patterns with great skill and taste.

Round their necks and arms they wore various chains and ornaments, and their ears and ankles were of course similarly decorated; but I am happy to say no unsightly nose-ring disfigured their countenances, nor do I think Kafir women ever wear them.

We parted from our beauties with regret, and I was quite grateful to them for breaking the monotony of the journey, which was not further enlivened by any attractive incident, or rendered interesting by any special feature of landscape until sunset.

After that, of course we could see no more, and I was not sorry when my husband rode up to tell me we should arrive in a few minutes at Mrs. Barnett's hospitable house at Ibéka.

Mr. Barnett is a trader "of credit and renown," and his wife is much liked for her gentle, amiable manner and hospitable character. She was now standing outside the door to welcome us, and, giving me her arm, assisted me most tenderly into the house, as I was too stiff and cramped to do more than totter along. The children were carried in fast asleep, and dear little Henry's slumber was so sweet and deep that all the bustle around failed to awake him.

A blazing fire was burning on the hearth, and in the kind faces all around and the bright smiles which greeted us, we felt the true atmosphere of home.

We were glad to sit down at once to the comfortable tea provided for us, and did justice to the delicious bread and butter which tasted all the sweeter from comparison with poor Mrs. Hahn's. The knowledge, too, that both were made by the fair fingers of the handsome young lady who was good enough to wait upon us (instead of summoning their Kafir servants), did not tend to lessen our enjoyment.

When the meal was over, good Mrs. Barnett, in compassion at my weary looks, offered to show me to my room: and, tired out with the fatigue and monotony of the day, the children, nurse, and I, were soon all fast asleep.

I hope my husband and his escort fared as well, but fear the wagon must have proved a scanty shelter, as the night was intensely cold, and ushered in a most miserable-looking day.

While dressing for breakfast I heard the sound of horses' hoofs outside, and a clatter which announced the arrival of additional guests.

A few moments after my husband came to tell me that Major Elliot [2] had just arrived, with one of the sons of Colonel Eustace; bringing kind messages from Mrs. Eustace, on the chance of meeting us here.

The whole party now assembled for breakfast, but I was glad when it was over, as poor Mrs. Barnett was perfectly besieged by applications for tea and coffee, and I do not believe she had a single mouthful herself, as a baby sat upon her lap the whole time.

I fervently hoped a time would come in which I should be able to return her kindness, and little knew how soon that opportunity would arise, still less that my pleasure at receiving her would be saddened by the fact that she and her family came to us as refugees, and that heavy sorrow and anxiety would sorely dim the visit they would pay to the Idutywa Reserve, our little home in the Transkei.

To that unknown home my thoughts now eagerly wandered, for only one more stage now intervened between us and Idutywa, and I was impatient to be off.

I looked out from the door to see what kind of place we were in, but "drizzling rain did fall," and a chilly mist enveloped every- thing.

How little did any of us guess how soon that dreary table-land would be covered with tents; that the stir and bustle of a military camp would animate dull Ibéka; and that the heroes of Isandlhana would be frequent guests at Mrs. Barnett's hospitable dwelling; doubtless appreciating the very pretty and pleasant Miss G——s as a welcome *douceur* in the midst of their monotonous life.

"Roses of the Wilderness," I called them; and I trust, roses not born *to waste their sweetness on the desert air.*

But we must now bid *adieu* to our kind hosts; for a weary trek awaits us before we can reach home; and it is Sunday morning, and we do not wish to delay the family prayers which are await-

2. Now Major Elliot, C.M.G.

ing our departure. Major Elliot and young Mr. Eustace left at the same time, and soon we say farewell to hospitable Ibéka.

I remember nothing about the last stage of our journey, except the bitter weather and the lonely, dreary appearance of everything.

The cold was such a contrast to the warmth of the preceding days, that we felt it all the more, and I shivered with ague, while the children "coughed and snoze "(as poor Henry said), and wished the weary journey over.

We could not venture to halt and make a cup of tea to warm us, as the oxen were so exhausted that the only chance of their taking us safely home, was never to allow them to stop. One poor animal had already died, and the others toiled sullenly along, looking as miserable as everything around.

We found biscuits very cold comfort, but I kept up my spirits by the thought that Mrs. Cumming would be certain to have a blazing fire and hot meal ready for us at the end of our journey, as we had taken the precaution of despatching an orderly to tell that lady at what hour we might confidently be expected to arrive.

As we toiled along a wretched road, my husband eagerly begged me to "look out," as we should see our home in a moment.

Of course I strained my eyes in the direction indicated, but could detect nothing like a house.

Presently I saw what at first I supposed to be some rough kind of fortification, but which was in reality the sod wall surrounding the garden of the magistrate; the house itself appearing as we mounted to higher ground, and some other roof being dimly discernible, which Edward said was that of our own little abode.

Mr. Cumming's residence was well built and a fair size, but looked cold and dreary on that bleak winter afternoon, and the whole aspect of the place was most forlorn and miserable.

Our home at Idutywa

CHAPTER 17

First sight of Home

No words can describe how my heart sank within me at the prospect of mouldering away my existence in this frightful solitude!

A dreary vista of years unmarked by any change, and of days passed in one monotonous round of neverending duty, rose before me, while at a glance I seemed to recall the happy years spent in my father's home; the ever-varying society gathered at almost every meal about his generous table; the gay and loving family circle, full of youth and animation; the beautiful mother, with, her aristocratic air and charming manner, and the father, whose wit and spirits never flagged; all these rose before me. Why had I been given this love of music, this passion for everything refined and beautiful, only to be tortured by a living death in this dreary desert, where I could never look on the face of any who had loved me in childhood, or hear so much as the song of a bird?

In one dark moment I seemed to suffer the agony of years, and my heart literally ached with real, physical pain.

But my good angel returned, in the thought of my children's love; no, come what might, I would not succumb.

I would find cheerfulness and sunshine in working for them; and while I had their sweet faces to look upon, I would not say all beauty was gone out of my life; I would read everything that came in my way, and keep my heart and brain alive with the echo of the distant world, though I could not share its glorious activity.

With one great effort I put the trial aside (in the cupboard where we all hide our skeletons), swallowed the "bullet in my throat," as little Harry would say, and ran determined to greet my future with a smile.

A very goodnatured–looking elderly gentleman now came forward and welcomed me to Idutywa, and my husband told me this was Mr. Cumming.

At the same moment I caught sight of a white lady standing in the dark at the back of the hall, and as the gentleman said she was Mrs. Cummings, I went up to her and took her hand.

Next morning I was charmed to find sunshine brightening the room. My spirits rose immediately and, eager to see how the landscape looked by daylight, I flew to the window and peeped behind the curtain, only to recoil at the sight which presented itself. Lady readers will sympathise with me when I say that, instead of the beautiful scenery I expected, I came suddenly face to face with the carcase of a sheep which had been hung just outside my window!

I thought this kind of thing was making the Transkei needlessly repulsive, and resolved to do my best to get into our own little cottage as rapidly as possible.

As soon as breakfast and prayers were over, I was up to my eyes in business. The first thing I had to do was to engage a washerwoman ("laundress" I cannot by any possible stretch of politeness venture to call her); secondly, to engage a couple of Kafir girls to assist Mrs. Gog in the housework; and it was quite ten o'clock before I could go and have a peep at our house, which I was of course dying to see.

At this moment I caught sight of a Kafir dancing in the veranda as if he had taken leave of his senses.

On inquiring the cause of this performance I was told that he was an animated mangle, and was ironing the table and bed linen which had just come from the wash!!

Imagine my dismay, fair readers, when I was told our clothes would simply be rough-dried at the river, and that there was not a creature who could starch or iron in the whole country! [1]

Mrs. Gog now reassured me by promising that if she might be invested with full authority and responsibility, she would undertake to get laundry-work, baking, and everything else done without any serious trouble to myself. I willingly acceded to this request, and the machinery of our little household worked smoothly and merrily until stopped and broken by the destroying angel of war.

These arrangements and engagements having all been satisfactorily completed, I put on my hat and dashed off to see our new home.

As soon as I had passed through the garden gate, I found myself in the midst of a most animated scene. The sunshine seemed to enliven everybody, and all were at work with a will.

Two distinct caravans were engaged, one in removing furniture, &c., from our house, the other in taking our possessions towards it. Groups of Kafirs, from neighbouring *kraals*, gathered round in interest and curiosity, and I confess to a feeling of anxiety as to the safety of our property, which was being unpacked on the open *veldt*. However, my husband assured me I need have no apprehensions; nor did we lose anything of value.

Edward now told me, that in spite of the precautions we had taken to purchase a small amount of furniture, he feared we had too much, and that it would be simply impossible to stow everything away.

I was myself reminded of the Vicar of Wakefield's famous family picture, when I looked at the tiny cottage, which was smaller than my utmost imagination had pictured it; but I had faith in the good genius of order, and felt certain I should find a place for everything in time.

The little cabin contained six rooms: a kitchen, a dining-room, two bedrooms, and two very miniature "*stoep*-rooms," as they are called at the Cape. (Small rooms stolen out of each end of the veranda.)

We fitted up one of these as a store-room, and the other made a tiny spare room; very convenient for gentlemen, as it was

1. I afterwards found this was quite a mistake.

entered from the *stoep* (veranda), and had no communication with any other room in the house.

I was delighted to get home, and anxious to take possession that night, if possible, but innumerable difficulties presented themselves to baffle this hope in every direction.

Chapter 18

The Lull before the Storm

However, these difficulties were overcome at last, and my husband and I had the pleasure of receiving our children at home on the Friday; having gone there ourselves the previous day. Until then we remained at the magistrate's, and were, I fear, compelled to treat our hosts rather cavalierly; as we were obliged to devote the greater part of each day to the arrangement of our own house, feeling anxious to relieve Mrs. Cumming of our presence as rapidly as possible. This lady had other guests in the house, and I had not yet had time to think the Transkei dull.

On the Monday two missionaries arrived at teatime, and as I had never in my life before even spoken to one, I was anxious to see what they would do, and hear what they had to say.

They were dressed with scrupulous care in clerical black, and I thought must have very good wives, for I'm sure no one at home could get up shirt-fronts more irreproachably.

Politics and prayers occupied the evening! I rather liked those missionaries after all,—and yet and yet—No, Mrs. Prichard, be charitable and go to sleep, and depend upon it, you will like them better in the morning.

They departed, however, directly after (not before) breakfast, but returned on the following evening, another gentleman also joining us at supper.

The latter was a well-known magistrate; a very eloquent man, thoroughly up in Kafir politics and affairs. We had a most interesting evening, and I was astonished to find this gentleman seemed as well versed in all the ramifications of Kafir kindred as we should be about our own. I wondered if I should ever be equally learned, and able to distinguish one black face from another. Meanwhile I found my own domestics quite bewildering enough, and concluded to solve the problem of household affairs, before venturing into the wider field of political economy.

These guests were all pleasant enough, but the following evening I had the honour of sitting at the table with a couple of Dutch farmers, who, judging from their manner and appearance, must have come from very upcountry indeed!

They had lost their horses, and were in a state of great excitement, describing their sorrows to the magistrate in such a graphic way that it was quite easy to follow the thread of their story by the help of one's distant remembrance of German.

They made such noises over their food! eating and drinking like ogres. I felt almost frightened once or twice of being "bolted "by way of a *bonne-bouche* at the close of the meal, and was glad my husband was there to protect me.

My private opinion is, that they were the lineal descendants of the great Fee-Fo-Fum! and that had not the magistrate plied them incessantly with provisions of a solid and satisfying nature, they would have chopped us all into mincemeat!

At the conclusion of the meal I was thankful to make my escape, and Edward and I took up our quarters for the first time in our own home, sitting up late for a cosy little supper, which we had great fun in preparing ourselves (as no servants were yet in the house), and which we thoroughly enjoyed after the carpentering and upholstery upon which we had been engaged all the evening.

The next visitors who arrived at Idutywa, were Colonel Eustace and Major Elliot, who appeared the following day. We were still somewhat in a state of chaos, and I'm not quite sure if we were able to supply them with chairs; however, I remember there was a table in the room, round which we gathered and looked at photographs, but whether we sat upon boxes, or on the floor, Oriental fashion, I'm sure I don't know.

These visitors departed next morning, and we enjoyed a quiet Sunday, followed by four equally peaceful days; which however, proved to be—only the lull before the storm!

CHAPTER 19

The Harbinger of the Storm

On Friday, the 10th August, our little household was apparently in a state of security; settled down into a routine which might have endured for years, and certainly never dreaming that we were already on the brink of a volcano; sitting beside a mine ready to explode at any moment; and that even now the harbinger of the storm was on his way to warn us of approaching danger.

My husband and I were just congratulating ourselves upon the comfortable appearance of everything around, when a gentle tap tap upon the door announced a visitor.

I was soon shaking hands with a lively little man, possessed of a cheery voice and genial manner, who was called Doctor S——.

We begged our friend to sit down, but he was in such a state of excitement that it was some time before we could induce him to do so.

I brought him a cup of tea, and Mrs. Gog appeared with other beverages; but he would touch neither until he had told us his grand piece of intelligence.

Shorn of the terrors with which the worthy doctor invested it, the facts amounted to this: a quarrel between some Fingoes and Gcalekas had ended in a "free fight," which had seriously disturbed the equanimity of the surrounding district.

Of course it was not pleasant to know that people were killing each other within a few miles of us, and I involuntarily clasped baby a little closer in my arms as I listened; but at the same time we were not going to make our new-found home miserable about such an apparent trifle, and fear we must plead guilty to "chaffing" the doctor rather unmercifully about the perils he might have to encounter during his ride home.

I must, however, confess to slight qualms when this Job's comforter had departed; especially when I reflected that on the following Monday my husband would leave home for an official tour, and I could not help hoping the opposing forces would be polite enough to suspend hostilities until his return.

I am happy to say this was the case, and everything went on quietly until Sunday, the 19th instant, when accounts of more serious disturbances were brought to the magistrate by a German trader. My husband had however, returned by this time, and I was so thankful for that blessing, that I did not allow myself to be worried by any bad news, and our household at any rate maintained its usual routine and regularity.

This continued for one more happy, and too short week, which slipped quickly away; marked by no special incident except the appearance of a sweetheart for Mrs. Gog!

This interesting arrival rejoiced in the name of Budge,- Billy Budge!

Never shall I forget that name! for, from the time that provoking man first invaded the haven of our home, its serenity departed, and I had the privilege henceforth of studying my—I beg pardon—Billy's Johanna, in the unexpected light of romance.

One Saturday evening Mrs. Gog appeared, all giggles—stay, that doesn't sound pretty—all smiles and blushes, anxious for my ever ready sympathy, and dying to tell me what had occurred.

I soon gathered that Mr. William Budge had been a friend of the departed Mr. Gog, who had been kind enough to retire many years since from this mundane scene, which he had persisted in regarding solely from a festive point of view.

After living entirely upon his (then young), wife's earnings for years, he had drunk himself gracefully—(disgracefully I should say)—into the grave; having led the life of "a perfect gentleman, doing nothing but eat, drink and sleep all day!"

This was a verdict pronounced upon some similar character by a servant of ours in the West Indies; but I must say I could not endorse the eulogium, as I did not consider the individual mentioned, worthy of even the last syllable of that much abused, but nevertheless honourable title, of gentleman.

I was pleased to hear a kind friend had appeared to take an interest in the widow, but may be excused for cherishing a secret hope that the courtship might be of somewhat a protracted nature!

CHAPTER 20

Arrival of the first Refugee

I was quite interested in this little bit of romance; but now Cupid must fly away and give place to Mars, who will be the presiding genius of the whole following week.

Monday, the 27th August, dawned bright and clear; but *before the dews of morn had fled* darkness had gathered over our horizon, and in the gloomy distance loomed the first dull thunder clouds of war.

One might have thought that missionaries; apostles of faith and love, and soldiers of Christ, would be (at any rate next in order to the earthly soldier), the very last to abandon their position: the first to rely upon the good faith of black neighbours among whom they had lived for years, and the foremost in courage; knowing that even if their lives were sacrificed, it would be at no unworthy shrine,—and that one or two examples of heroism and loyalty would do more to increase the Kafir's faith in our greatness as a nation than reams upon reams of sermons and tall talk.

One might even have ventured to suppose that for the sake of righteous influence upon the morale of the poor white Christians around them, they would convert each mission station into a rallying point and centre, where every timid nature would seek comfort and courage; where the warriors should be prayed for, the wounded nursed, the women encouraged, and the children fed; so that, come what might, their Kafir converts should say, We Christians were soldiers indeed, and willing to die for Him

84

who had so willingly died for us.

Alas! alas! I dip my pen in tears, and those tears of shame and sorrow, as I recall how little loyalty, either to heaven or man, was exhibited at this juncture.

Verily war is a crucible which brings all the dross to the surface, and only the purest gold can bear the test, and emerge, brighter and nobler, for the trial. Under that fiery ordeal the worst and the best passions in our nature seem to rise in unrestrained energy, and only prayerful trust in One mightier than ourselves can nerve the heart and calm the brain in that fierce conflict. The conventionalities of ordinary life are put aside for the time, and you see each character to the very core. Appalled, you shudder at some painful revelations; but on the other hand, you will see those who under ordinary circumstances modestly conceal the worth and courage of their nature, quietly come forward, and without a thought of themselves, act as the true and noble heroes all are capable of becoming, if they will but obey the impulse of the Divine nature, which is the glorious heritage of man.

But my mission is to sew, not to preach; and while I am engaged in this peaceful occupation, sitting on a low chair in our pretty veranda, I become suddenly aware of a shade on the ground before my feet. At the same time a would-be-bland voice is inquiring if I am "Mistress Prichard," and if my "good man is within."

I was about to answer in the affirmative, when I remembered my husband had warned me of the expected arrival of a missionary, famous for his very long tongue, and very small talk; and knowing Edward was hard at work, I was Scotchman enough to reply by asking the name of my interrogator. [1]

As this corresponded with that of the individual mentioned above, I thought the kindest thing I could do was to keep him away from Edward as long as possible.

All my efforts were, however, in vain; and after exhausting

---

1. Is there such a word in the dictionary? If there is not, there "oughter," so I do not withdraw it.

every blandishment in my power, I had the mortification of seeing my friend depart to the office-tent, to give the busy engineer the benefit of all the horrors he had been inflicting upon me.

As I sat and stitched and listened in amusement, (if not in interest), to the poor man, I could not help mentally comparing him to Edgar Allen Poe's immortal Raven; for *never-more* seemed to echo at the conclusion of every sentence, and his lamentations were worthy of a Jeremiah.

In vain I attempted to cheer him, or inspire him with an atom of courage. He evidently thought there was not the slightest charm in civil war, unless we all enjoyed ourselves thoroughly, by making everybody else as miserable as possible!

I listened politely as long as I could, but at last my risible faculties were too much for me; and when we arrived at the utmost pitch of horror, and attained the most thrilling point in the narrative, I could no longer maintain my gravity, and peal after peal of laughter rang upon the clear morning air.

I thought it quite sufficient to face these horrors quietly when they came, and did not feel it my duty to advance nine-tenths of the way to meet them; so finding his eloquence wasted, the unhappy Raven retired, evidently looking upon me as a hopeless case!

I now gathered up my work, and summoning Johanna, gave her sundry directions with regard to dinner, &c.

These directions had to be of a somewhat vague and elastic nature. I had heard that refugees were pouring into the "Reserve" from every point of the compass, and had therefore to instruct Mrs. Gog to be ready for any emergency; to purchase everything that was brought to the door, and to be prepared to accommodate the greatest number of guests we could possibly manage to stow away.

I had hardly finished giving these directions when various visitors arrived. Several gentlemen dined with us, and each vied with the other in piling up the agony as high as possible.

Each had just come through hair-breadth escapes of the most harrowing interest and dangerous nature; and I tried hard to be a gentle Desdemona, and sympathize with our heroes.

As these Othellos had however, chiefly achieved distinction in that discretion which is the better part (?) of valour, and as their appetites seemed rather increased than diminished by the peril which surrounded us, I thought practical rather than romantic sympathy would be the best thing to offer!

They found the cup of consolation in copious draughts of Bass's ale, and by the time some fritters (for which Mrs. Gog was particularly celebrated) had arrived, our friends had wisely resolved to banish our anxieties for awhile, and enjoy the sunshine of today without overclouding it by the shadow of tomorrow!

CHAPTER 21

Our last Sunday at home

Next day, more refugees arrived; among them the Barnett family from Ibéka with the exception of Mr. Barnett himself, who courageously remained at home to defend his property, relying valiantly upon the good faith of his Kafir neighbours, in which he was not disappointed!

I now began to feel our house sadly too small, and the table arrangements quite inadequate to these new claims.

However, I retired to my room, and locking the door, held on to my head with both hands until I had evolved a plan which promised to meet the difficulties of the situation.

I then departed to the dining-room; summoned the united forces of the establishment, and ordered the crimson carpet (laid down so carefully only a few days before), to be taken up again and removed altogether. I then took away all the books and ornaments which were most dear to me, and banished the pretty round table to my own room.

I now sent for the largest tables in the house, and fitted them together into one great, square table, which almost occupied the entire room. All this completely destroyed the beauty and symmetry of the house; but this was the time to think of others, not of ourselves; and we were grateful at being permitted the privilege of helping those in distress.

I now directed the table to be kept always ready for sixteen people, and ordered plenty of cold provisions to be at hand, so that something could be offered at a moment's notice to any guests "who might arrive between meals, and who might be weary and faint from long travelling and fasting.

So much for the Commissariat Department!

Now I must think how to manage sleeping accommodation for my guests; and in fact I began to feel like a landlady; having all the trouble of keeping an hotel, only—without the pay.

Of course the little "*stoep*-room" must be the bachelors' quarters as usual, but I can arrange a bed for a young lady in one of our two dormitories inside the house, by taking the children into our own room. The young lady will have to submit to nurse's company at night; but I will put their beds on opposite sides of the room, and nurse's good humour will keep the poor girl's spirits up.

Every evening at nine o'clock, nurse and I will turn all the gentlemen out of the house for a smoke on the *stoep*, and while they are out of the way we will push aside the tables and make shake-downs all round the dining-room, and they must all use the bachelors' den as a dressing-room. As for servants, they will have to sleep in the kitchen; and should we be very much crowded, I can arrange hammocks in the veranda, and put blankets on the floor of the passage; but meanwhile we have camp bedsteads enough, and any amount of linen, so no one need be uncomfortable just yet.

This result of my cogitations made me quite happy again, and I was glad to have so much to do that I had no time to feel frightened or indeed think of the war at all, except from a practical point of view. We really got through the week very well; Miss G. and I spending our mornings in the veranda as quietly as if nothing of an unusual nature was going on. Pretty Miss G. busy at her "Little Wanzer;" engaged in hemming new table-cloths and serviettes for me, and I, usually acting tailor at my cutting-out table, while the ravens came and fed us with news. I told all our guests they were welcome to everything we had to offer, on one condition;—that no groans were allowed. So everyone did his best to tell his story in the most amusing way, and nothing but harmony and mirth reigned in our household.

After a day or two the excitement somewhat subsided, and by the Friday afternoon everything seemed so quiet, that Mrs. Barnett and her family returned to Ibéka; the Gosses (afterwards killed in action), and some other people departed; and by Sunday, the 2nd September, things had all but returned to their normal condition at Idutywa, and on the Sunday afternoon a little service was held at the magistrate's and attended by quite a congregation of white people.

The whole of the following week passed away quietly, and we went on steadily with our duties. Several people came to see us, and I do not remember any meal at which some guest was not present. We banished painful topics as much as possible, thinking it more prudent to do so; as our Kafir servants could hear every word said in the dining-room, and we did not feel sure whether their ignorance of our language was assumed or not. Still, all feeling of security was gone, and we felt a surprise might come at any moment. I sat resolutely at my needlework in the veranda, but it was rather a strain upon one's nerves to do so.

In front of our house was a piece of ground which we hoped to convert into a flower garden; but during these troublous times no one could be induced to fence it for any consideration. We had therefore no means of shutting out the public, and as the nearest way to the magistrate's was along a path which ran side by side with our veranda; I saw and heard a good deal which I kept to myself, but which made me uneasy.—When we first arrived at Idutywa, the natives would pass our house respectfully; walking on the side of the path farthest away from me, and almost invariably addressing me as "*Inkŏs;*" their whole demeanour expressing deference and respect.

I had always returned these salutations with civility, and the women often brought their babies to show me, and seemed pleased if I noticed them in any way. Now all was changed; the men swaggered past me with a most insolent air; often brushing my dress carelessly with their *assegais*, for all were armed to the teeth, and displayed their weapons as much as possible.—I thought the most loyal thing to do was to bear it patiently, and sit quietly until they were out of sight, when I would resume my work; but it was a great effort to do so.

Some would even laugh and nod; first at each other and then at the house, and I fancied these significant looks meant, "Oh! yes, my fine lady-chief (*Inkōs*), these pretty things belong to you for a few more days, but they will soon enough change hands"!

When these insults became too unbearable I would go for a walk with my husband, to shake off the nervous impression. Just about this time the little station at Idutywa was enlivened by a visit from Captain Fraser, (of the telegraph department), who pitched his busy and pretty camp just above our house. Of course we all went to pay him a visit, and I was quite interested in all the curious things he showed us.

Captain Fraser was very kind in explaining everything in the most charming way, but I never could swallow even the smallest dose of science, and should be just as contented if the earth were square, or rested on a tortoise's back; still I liked to look at the water in the glasses and dip my finger into it, and know that everything in the place could go off if it chose!

I was also charmed with Captain Fraser's costume, which was made entirely of dark brown leather. It was very becoming, perfectly adapted to the bush; and I did nothing but beg my husband to procure a similar dress all the way home.

Of course the work was being hurried on as fast as possible, as it would be invaluable should any serious disturbance occur; and we all looked lovingly at the telegraph poles, for they seemed a link to civilisation, and we felt very much safer when they were all put up. We went to say goodbye to our friend when he left, and as I looked at the people striking the tents and preparing for departure, how little I guessed that the next camp I should see would be our own; that one dear child would die in a tent, and another little one be born in a tent; and that the time would come when I should look back upon our little cottage at Idutywa as a palace of luxury and paradise of peace; and that all these changes would occur before that line of telegraph was finished!

We certainly had no reason to complain of feeling dull at present; and the little bustle Captain Fraser's camp created had not yet subsided, when we received official information that his Excellency the Governor, Sir Bartle Frere, and his suite, were about to honour the Transkei with a visit; and my husband received a command to proceed immediately to Butterworth, to receive his Excellency's instructions. Of course this grand piece of intelligence plunged the whole station into the wildest state of excitement; and we wondered what effect the spectacle of a quiet, elderly gentleman in a shooting-coat would have upon the minds of the natives.

What would we not have given for the presence of a brigade of troops,—a military band,—gorgeous uniforms,—splendid equipages—elephants—*nautch*-girls—Hengler's Circus—anything or everything to astonish the natives. When would something happen to show the Kafirs we really were big people? How can they form the smallest estimate of England's greatness from the scattered handfuls of white people divided from each other by distance, and connected by no ties of affection, whom they contemptuously permitted to dwell among them? All I know is, I am exceedingly grateful to them for not despatching us long ago, for that they could have massacred us with the greatest ease is a fact which no one acquainted with the country will dispute.

My husband left home on Friday, the 14th September, and I feared he might not return for several days; I expected to be very dull, and determined to amuse myself with a good house-cleaning during his absence. Mrs. Gog's energies had lately been chiefly occupied with the cuisine, and the house was really looking rather black! I thought an air of neglect would impress the Kafir servants with the idea that we did not expect to remain there long; so partly from loyalty to good Queen Victoria, and partly from respect to my own love of order, we cleared the decks and prepared for action. All that Saturday morning we scrubbed, and dusted, and polished, and sang, and laughed, and scolded; until we were almost too tired to eat the hasty luncheon which was all I cared for as my husband was away. After dinner, feeling our work was done, nurse went to lie down in her own room; I locked the front door, took a book, and imitated her example. The Kafir servants took the children out for a walk, and nurse and I never heard the arrival of a visitor, who was no less a personage than Major Elliot.

After ineffectual attempts to make himself heard, he departed to the magistrate's in despair.

He returned, however, in about a quarter of an hour, and this time the knocking at the front door fortunately awoke me.

Startled and nervous, and still half asleep; I was on the point of opening the door, when good nurse pushed me back into the dining-room, and ushered in Major Elliot. We were soon laughing about his unsuccessful attempts to attract our attention; and when I began to feel a little more awake I made the usual inquiry as to whether he was travelling "up" or "down" country." How could I ask such a stupid question?

"Down," of course; he was on his way to pay his respects to his Excellency at Butterworth, but would remain at Idutywa until the Monday. I knew the magistrate's house was full to overflowing, and that he would not care to go there; here was a dilemma; what was I to do?

Nurse looked "Yes!" from the kitchen door, and I ventured to ask if Major Elliot would like to take up his quarters in the little *stoep*-room for the next day or two. He at first declined, and after a short visit went off to look after his horses. I now sent for Magog, the tall orderly who had been left behind to take care of us all; and requested him to go and tell the Major that my husband had left a special message begging him to make use of the little outside room if he should arrive during his absence; and he delivered his message so diplomatically, that in a few moments he returned with valise and saddlebags, and said their owner would be very pleased to accept my husband's invitation.

How glad nurse and I were that we had got all our cleaning over early in the day;—now we had almost nothing to do, but see that the evening meal was all right and await the return of our guest. He and the children all came in good time for tea, and little Henry was very much gratified at being allowed to sit up to "late dinner," as he called it, and behaved with the utmost dignity and propriety.

When tea was over, we were glad to chat beside the fire, for the evenings were now very cold; and I wondered how the Governor would endure the hardship of sleeping in a tent that night!

I was very tired after my morning's work; and kind Major Elliot, perhaps pitying my sleepy looks, soon called for Mrs. Gog to come and lock him out, and departed, "to have a pipe with Fraser."

Nurse and I were most grateful for this considerate piece of thoughtfulness, and soon retired to rest. I was asleep in a moment, but awoke about midnight in some alarm, as I heard voices talking, and fancied at first the Kafirs had surprised us, and that Magog and the other orderly had come to announce the fact. In another moment however, I recognized the voices as those of Major Elliot and Captain Fraser, and guessed correctly that, finding the air cold on the *veldt*, they had preferred the cosy snugness of the cabin, and were smoking in the little *stoep*-room outside. I could distinguish the voices, but fortunately could not hear a word they said, as the wall of the house intervened; knowing all was right, I was just composing myself off to sleep again, when I heard a low whistle in the veranda; and at the same moment I heard three gentlemen's voices exclaiming simultaneously, "Who's there?" in rather military tones.

Recognizing my husband's signal whistle, I felt quite happy, and thoroughly enjoyed the fun; only hoping they would not fire upon each other all round before they had found out their mistake.

A hearty chorus of laughter reassured me on this head, and by the time I had donned my dressing-gown and opened the front door, the three supposed burglars were shaking hands in the most cordial manner!—It seemed the Governor had been kind enough to release my husband, telling him to go home and take care of his wife, and return on Monday; my husband, nothing loath, galloped away; and on arriving at home was startled at seeing a light in the window of Bachelor's Den; however, he imagined that some refugee was quartered there; and thought nothing of it until he heard two men's voices.

This alarmed him; and, fearing something wrong, he was just prepared to give them rather a warm reception. But when the supposed assassins heard his low warning whistle, which was intended for my ears alone—surprised in their turn, and suspicious of everything and everybody in those anxious times,—they braced themselves for the expected foe, and prepared a doubly warm welcome for my poor husband! However, all recognized each other at the first word, and no harm was done.—I was delighted to see Edward again so soon, especially on Major Elliot's account; as I feared he would find Sunday a fearfully dull day to drag through, with only women and children to entertain him.

This Sunday was the last my husband and I ever spent together in our dear little cabin, and it was rather an eventful one. Major Elliot was a delightful visitor, making himself thoroughly at home, and the day was further marked by our reception of a distinguished guest! The individual in question was Gangelizwe, paramount chief of the Tembus, and son-in-law to Kreli, chief of the Gcalekas, against whom we so shortly afterwards proclaimed war. Major Elliot was Resident with him, and generally responsible for his good behaviour and loyalty to the British Government.

Many were the jokes about the major's "baby," and I was on the tiptoe of expectation, when we were told that the great chief, with a retinue of three hundred warriors (among them a real, live witchdoctor), had actually arrived in the Idutywa Reserve and was awaiting Major Elliot's wishes! I flew to put on some ornaments to brighten my black dress, and charged nurse to bring in the refreshments selected by our dusky guest, as I knew she would enjoy being present at the interview.

I then awaited the arrival of our chief, who appeared in a few minutes, escorted with due respect by Major Elliot and my husband. After the first compliments were over, and our guest was seated; we asked him what he would take to drink.

"Brandy, brandy! "he cried; "no water, no water; brandy very good"

It was brought, with wine for the two gentlemen, and he absolutely grinned with delight, when it was poured with no measured hand into a large tumbler.

"More, more! "he kept exclaiming until the glass was nearly full. He now called for a tumbler of water, and then, having first bowed politely to the three palefaces, he tossed off the glass of perfectly "neat" brandy at a draught, drinking the whole of the water the moment after, to get as it were two glasses for one! He did not take any more, and the brandy had no visible effect upon him. While he was eating and drinking I found time to scrutinize our visitor, and could hardly believe the dreadful stories I had heard about this handsome-looking man; there was nothing repulsive in his countenance, and his expression was rather sweet and gentle; beautiful teeth and the smile of a child. The back of the head was not particularly good, but I cannot say it was particularly bad, and for once I felt, physiognomy and phrenology were at fault.

While we were talking to our guest, a curious-looking white man came through the kitchen; and after lingering for a moment at the door, entered the dining-room in a strange, stealthy manner, and crouched down upon the floor behind Gangelizwe's chair. The chief sat exactly opposite to me. Major Elliot and my husband occupied chairs on my right and left hand, and we three sat facing the beforementioned door; which was therefore behind Gangelizwe.

The man entered the house with such an air of composure, that we imagined he was an interpreter to the chief, and that Gangelizwe had sent for him; and the odd position behind his chair seemed only an expression of humility and respect. We therefore said nothing, and had not the slightest idea anything was wrong, until Gangelizwe, on turning, and for the first time seeing the man, started up, his face absolutely white with terror, the muscles working with mingled rage and fear, and his whole countenance presenting the most repulsive appearance, it has ever been my lot to see.

"Tell that man go away, away, away!" he shouted, almost foaming with rage and terror; and now it flashed upon us that the man had nothing to do with the chief, and that Gangelizwe actually suspected us of having introduced an assassin to stab him in the back, while he sat peacefully partaking of our hospitality!!

Such an impression was the very last thing any white person in the Transkei would have wished for at that crisis, and it required tact and time to obliterate the disagreeable effect produced. Of course the interloper was speedily sent about his business, but what that business was—who he was, and whence he came—will ever remain a mystery.

Major Elliot or my husband would have inquired further into the matter, but could not very well leave me with Gangelizwe, who was in the wildest state of excitement; besides, they saw the man was not quite himself, and evidently harmless, his only object in entering our house uninvited having been a motive of curiosity, and a wish to see the celebrated chief. We therefore let him depart in peace, and concentrated our united efforts in the attempt to soothe the irritation of our insulted guest.

The secret consciousness that, in a few more days, our lives might be at his mercy perhaps tended to sharpen our wits; remembering that *Music hath charms to soothe the savage breast*, I whispered a request to Mrs. Gog to bring her musical box. Thoroughly entering into the spirit of the thing, she quietly withdrew, and speedily returned with the little instrument which had so often been the "plague of my life," but on this occasion proved our best friend. Gangelizwe looked up at her entrance, (he evidently admired her very much, and indeed, her comely figure looked quite charming in her Sunday dress), but did not notice the box upon the table at his side, until it began to play..

Then his face was a study! It perfectly glowed with surprise and pleasure, and he looked with an air of bewilderment all about the room, and then at ourselves, for an explanation. I really think he fancied the house was bewitched, and am confident he would have summoned his band of warriors, witchdoctor and all, to his assistance, had not my husband carefully explained the mystery of the music.

Reassured, he now gave himself up to enjoyment, fondled the little instrument as if it had been a child, laid his head against it to hear better, and smiled at us with an expression, not merely of childish amusement, but of real, musical feeling! What a strange compound truly is this curious human nature, and how closely are the threads of good and evil mingled in the tangled web of character! How thankful we should be that we have for a Judge, One who will make tenderest allowance for the circumstances in which we have been placed; One who will so lovingly bring out the best, and eradicate the worst side of our nature; and who, by little and little, will surely purify every soul, and lead it gently into progressive states of happiness!

We were interested in our strange guest in spite of our prejudice against him, and did our best to treat him with the respect due to his rank, and the position he held as our ally. Imagine my dismay, therefore, when Edward, who cannot long restrain his passion for teasing me; answered a query made by Gangelizwe, as to whether a little statuette representing Purity was a figure of Queen Victoria! by the atrocious reply, "Oh! dear no! that is not an image of Queen Victoria! don't you see it is intended to represent my wife?"

Gangelizwe smiled and nodded at this abominable reply, and as I thought Kafir etiquette would be outraged if I administered the hearty box on the ear which my husband so richly deserved, I withdrew from the room; rather glad to avoid by this means a parting salute from Gangelizwe. The chief soon retired, but next morning, while we were having a seven o'clock breakfast, for the benefit of our travellers, he reappeared in a charming temper, and without attendants; and, thanking us for our trifling hospitality of the day before, said, with the air of a prince, that he had come to bid farewell to the kind lady-chief; he also inquired for Mrs. Gog, whom he evidently imagined to be my husband's other wife; and whom he treated with much deference and respect. I now walked with little Henry up to Captain Fraser's camp, whence Major Elliot, Gangelizwe, and my husband were to start for Butterworth, the halting-place of the Governor. The departure was really quite imposing, and the whole scene most animated and interesting: the three hundred mounted warriors, dressed in every variety of fantastic finery, the acme being attained in the witchdoctor's costume, [1] which was arranged in such a bewildering way that she looked more like an ostrich dressed up as a scarecrow than anything else!

However, they all possessed the beauty of fidelity, at all events; and therefore we looked upon them with interest in spite of their motley appearance.—Another animated scene was presented in the telegraph camp, and Idutywa seemed quite gay. When the procession was in perfect order, Major Elliot, my husband, and Gangelizwe, rode side by side at the head of the column; then followed Edward's escort of gentlemen, and these were again followed by "the three hundred," who rode three or four abreast. It was a pretty sight on that bright, frosty morning, but I barely saw it start, as I wished to return to the house, knowing it was just that hour in the day when the guiding hand of the mistress is most needed at the helm. It was a time when one did not much like the gentlemen of one's household to be away, but I comforted myself with the reflection that my husband was safe if we were not; and with the certainty that he would return the moment he could possibly get away.

---

1. This witchdoctor was killed and beheaded a few days after in one of the skirmishes; imagine the horror of our forces when they discovered the poor thing was a woman who had sacrificed her life in fidelity to her chief and to Queen Victoria!

CHAPTER 22

I lose my Rose-Coloured Spectacles

Next day, Tuesday, the 18th of September, Edward galloped up just in time for dinner, and on the Wednesday, Major El-liot appeared, and again took up his quarters in Bachelor's Den, leaving for Umtata the following day. We had a merry evening, sitting cosily round the fire; discussing the Governor's visit. My husband had had the honour of lunching with his Excellency on the Saturday, of dining with him on the Monday, and join-ing him at breakfast on the Tuesday morning, and had much appreciated his kindness and hospitality. I also sincerely thanked him for an act of thoughtful consideration which showed the kindness of his nature to great advantage. Sir Bartle Frere had gone up to one of the young men in my husband's escort, and inquired why he did not put on his overcoat, as the air was so bitterly keen.

"We have no overcoats, sir," replied the poor fellow in the most cheerful, uncomplaining way.

"No overcoats! "responded his Excellency in unutterable tones of commiseration and amazement; "this must be looked into at once."

And I am delighted to say the deficiency was speedily recti-fied. I thought this was so nice in the Governor, and must be excused for recording this little incident.

No other event of interest occurred until Friday of the same week, the 21st September, when Idutywa was again enlivened by the advent of a military-looking column of armed and mounted police (now called Cape Mounted Rifles), who appeared upon the hills south of our house about four o'clock in the afternoon. I flew for the children to see the "pretty soldiers," and my husband dashed off to ascertain who they were and whence they came. He soon returned with the agreeable information that the force consisted of one hundred men, under the command of an inspector. Several other officers were there with whom he was acquainted, and he went off to see them as soon as they had pitched their tents.

I may be pardoned for regarding the arrival of this force with some thankfulness and rejoicing, when I state that on the following morning, the 22nd of September, my husband would be obliged to leave home for several weeks, as he had received instructions from the Governor to proceed immediately to Umtata (the northern limit of the Transkei, and about a hundred miles away), to commence the work which Government had stopped the previous year on account of the supposed unsettled state of the country.

This had been during the term of Sir Henry Barkly's governorship, and if the country was not at that time in a fit state for the work, how much less was it now in a condition for such a thing! However, our duty was to obey; but I may be forgiven if I confess to a sad sinking at heart as I assisted in the preparations for my husband's departure, as my own state of health made a wagon journey a thing not to be thought of except under most urgent and pressing circumstances. This alone prevented our accompanying him, though could we have foreseen the calamities of the following week, we should of course have risked everything sooner than face a separation.

My readers will not wonder that my husband's anxiety about our safety was materially diminished at the arrival of so many armed white men at the Idutywa; and next morning he started in good spirits, after having presented to me the different officers, who all came to see us in the veranda, and gave me a kind welcome to the Transkei.

The senior officer was Inspector C——; Sub-inspectors Allan and J. Maclean, Mr. Hamilton, Mr. Cochrane, and Dr. Sharpe, the medical officer, were all there; and I felt very brave indeed with so many warriors to take care of us. But after the stir and bustle of their visit was over, the feeling of depression returned; and, for the first time in those troublous times, I could not rouse myself to look for the silver lining behind the cloud. My husband rallied me upon my fit of "blues," assured me the colour was not at all becoming, and asked if I had lost my rose-coloured spectacles, entreating me to "get up a smile "to speed him on his way. Fearing I was making myself disagreeable, I did manage to comply with this request, but my heart told me it was no vague foreboding, but a real presentiment of evil; which weighed down body and mind alike.

As the wagon in which my husband was travelling toiled slowly up the hill, little Henry and I toiled wearily after it, following as long as we could, until Edward, fearing we might lose our way, motioned to us to turn back. As we did so, the wagon disappeared; and something warned me that moment was our farewell to our happy home at Idutywa! So indeed it proved, for when my husband again visited the place, wife and children had fled, the station was deserted, and the little home upon which we had expended so much loving labour, was a wreck; a scene of chaos and confusion; tenanted by troops, desecrated by disorder, and only too perfect a monument to the angry god of war.—But I am anticipating.—This was Saturday, the 22nd of September.

CHAPTER 23

Declaration of War

Next day Captain Grant arrived, bringing up a gun which
Mr. C—— had sent for. And now indeed one would have
thought I ought to regain my courage; but no, a thunder cloud
seemed to oppress my soul, and I was so convinced something
disastrous was about to occur, that I devoted nearly the whole
of that lonely, dreary day to the task of arranging and destroying
papers; sorting and classifying everything into the state I should
least regret, should our house and possessions fall into the hands
of the enemy. I write this word for the first time, for it is only
today that we all face the fact that it is too late to draw back;
Colonel Eustace having left Kreli (equivalent to the departure
of an ambassador from an inimical Foreign Court), and I now
realize that henceforward I must be father and mother in one,
for my husband has gone on the very day of the declaration of
war, [1] and it is to me alone that our children must look for safety
and protection.

Every nerve must be controlled, and every effort concentrated upon the task; and this thought animated me with courage,
banishing the gloomy cloud which had too long oppressed me,
and many months passed away before it again returned.

Everything went on tolerably quietly until the Wednesday.
Captain Grant called before leaving on the Monday; and the
other officers were good enough to fulfil the promise exacted
by my husband, to come and cheer me up. Some refugees ar-

---

1. Unconsciously, of course.

rived, and I had a houseful of guests to entertain, and altogether my hands, feet and brain were all kept so busily employed that I had no time to feel nervous, or listen to the horrible stories which every newcomer had to relate.

Still it was uncomfortable to know that we were being surrounded by a cordon of foes, whose numbers we had no means of estimating, whose courage was undoubted, and whose arms and ammunition had been perhaps provided by some of the very traders now trembling about our doors. I gave them hospitality, but sympathy I could not summon; as, but for these men, we should not now be menaced by weapons equal, if not superior to our own.

Wednesday, the 26th of September, 1877, dawned bright and clear; and by the time I had finished my household duties, the atmosphere and sunshine were so utterly bewitching, that it was simply impossible to resist their attractions, and I really could not sit still in the house. We can always find an excuse for idleness, so I became suddenly seized with a conscientious fit of remorse, and conveniently remembered that I had not been to see Mrs. Cumming for more than a week. This duty must of course be performed at once, and summoning my little son as "*preux chevalier*," I put on my hat, and sallied forth.

I was somewhat surprised to find Mrs. Cumming in the garden. She greeted me very kindly, and told me that she and her lady-visitors had gone there to see the "police" start for a morning ride. Knowing the celebrated brothers Maclean would be some of the cavaliers in question, and being further aware that the whole country was charged with electricity which only required a touch to set it on fire, it was no wonder if we watched the departure of the column with some degree of excitement, and invested the whole affair with a colouring of interest almost amounting to romance.

This interest was heightened by the knowledge that the gun was to accompany the party, in charge of some members of the artillery corps which formed part of the force; and we all felt this morning ride would end in some collision with the opposing forces. Of course the little army looked "lovely," at least in the eyes of the women and children who regarded these gallant warriors (so soldier-like, with their handsome figures, upright bearing, and neat uniforms), as our defenders and champions; and I think had they known the amount of courage and heroism with which we credited them, they would scarcely have ventured to bring back a tale of defeat to one woman who that day admired and envied them.

But *he who fights and runs away, may live to fight another day*; and some who fled from the Guadana, lived to share gallantly in many a future fight; and in the heroic deeds of after-engagements to recover the prestige which the first shock and surprise of overwhelming numbers had for one short day somewhat dimmed. If we invested our heroes with so much valour, and gave them credit for so much power of resistance, it is small wonder if we began to feel rather unprotected after they were gone;—this was especially the case with myself, when I found that the two members of my husband's escort who had been left by him at Idutywa for our protection and defence, had, without a word of warning to me, gone off with the riding-party.

This was very provoking, and not quite right, but I made every allowance for the "chaff" they would have suffered from their comrades had they remained at home at ease, while others were dashing into the jaws of danger; and feeling that under similar circumstances I should probably have felt sorely tempted to do as they had done, I made up my mind to say nothing about it to my husband, and simply hope nothing serious would occur during their absence.

This hope was not however, realized; during the day refugees from all directions arrived at the Idutywa, and these were not merely people of our own colour and creed;—hundreds of Fingo families (our allies) poured into the Reserve, bringing with them flocks and herds, goods and chattels; until the quiet little place became a babel of confusion and disorder, and resembled a huge cattle-pen more than anything else.

Mr. Cumming was most kind to these poor people, had

rough sheds erected to shelter as many as possible, and did everything in his power to inspire them with confidence. In spite of this, they looked most miserable; turned out of their homes, and with but scanty prospects of ever seeing them again, and our own hearts ached as we witnessed their sufferings and felt their experience might be ours before many days had passed over our heads.

It was not a scene very suitable for a lady, especially one new to the country, and I was glad to remain in the house, and occupy myself in the preparation of linen, lint, and other comforts for the wounded who might too soon require our care. In this I was directed by the worthy, little doctor whom I have before mentioned, and with his advice and assistance, I converted the little *stoep*-room into a surgery, and placed there our medicine-chest, and every other appliance we could muster.

There I wasted oceans of sympathy and hours of fatiguing work, upon the victorious but wounded heroes, whom we expected every moment to return.—Morning passed, afternoon arrived, and evening changed into night; but still no trace or sign of our champions. At last, feeling it useless to sit up any longer, I lay down to rest, but it was impossible to sleep; for the incessant bleating of sheep, lowing of cattle, and tread of hurried feet, continued without intermission during the entire night.

Besides this, there were patrols and amateur sentinels of every description, going and coming so perpetually, and keeping so suspiciously close to the house, that I thought they were not much use, as Mrs. Gog and I would certainly have known had any danger menaced us at such very close quarters! One's own thoughts too were busy, and a thousand questions occupied one's brain. Where were the Imperial troops? had they yet crossed the frontier or landed at Mazeppa Bay? Would the police return before the Idutywa was invaded?

Where was my husband by this time?—Had he arrived safely at Umtata, or had he fallen into the hands of the enemy? All these anxious considerations kept one awake, and I was quite thankful when the first rays of daylight stole into the room, and

Mrs. Gog, who had passed an equally sleepless night, brought a cup of delicious coffee to recruit my exhausted energies.

CHAPTER 24

A Terrible Night

We dragged through the whole of that weary day of suspense somehow or other,—going mechanically about our duties, and careful to preserve the usual routine as rigidly as possible, but all interest in those duties was completely gone, and we simply ate to live. The children were as sweet as ever, and charmed with the bustle and stir about them, and their happiness was a solace amidst the distracting scene around, though their presence was an additional source of anxiety.

When they had gone to bed, I resumed my preparations for the wounded, working away under the direction of the little doctor, who looked as happy over our beautifully-fitted medicine-chest as a child over her first paintbox, but who found time to spare for a merry word with Mrs. Gog, who, too modest to sit down in the dining-room, and too excited to remain alone in the kitchen, (Kafir servants go home every night) leaned against the door, and watched our proceedings with the utmost sympathy and interest. Of course we were all "on the *qui-vive*" and ears and eyes alike seemed endowed with supernatural activity.

Our conversation was somewhat of an effort, and I was just feeling I could no longer keep up the strain, and must go away to be alone, when I heard a feeble knock at the front door, and in another moment a ghastly-looking spectre appeared on our threshold. I repeat—a spectre; for without the smallest wish to use a sensational word, I am compelled to apply this to the haggard, battle-stained figure, who stood in the darkness of our little hall, leaning on his gun for support, and looking too faint and feeble to enter the room. Was this the doughty champion who was to return flushed with success, to pour the tidings of victory into our delighted ears? Surely;—surely, it cannot be the omen of defeat, and yet, if all has gone well, why does he not announce the joyful news with a look of triumph, even if that look should be his last!

Before we recover our senses sufficiently to address this apparition, he, poor thing, tries to summon strength to speak to us, and in the feebly-uttered accents which come slowly and brokenly from his parched lip, I distinguish an apology for having left me without warning; an explanation that he thought they were only going for a morning ride, and now, in the consideration and delicacy of feeling which prompts him to report himself and tender this explanation before he has had so much as a drop of water to quench his thirst or wash away the dust and smoke of battle which makes him all but unrecognizable; I discern the courteous instinct of a gentleman, and see for the first time, that the phantom stranger, who looks so enormously tall and ghost-like in the darkness, is the gentle giant whom I introduced to my readers as "Magog."

My rapid glance of recognition shows me that poor Magog is all but fainting, so I merely smile and nod in reply, and make a dash for a chair with one hand while I signal with the other to nurse to bring food,—supper,—anything; as fast as she possibly can. While she flies to the pantry for bread and meat, the little doctor turns butler and opens the bottle of Bass which I produce hastily for our poor "phantom;" perhaps not the nicest or best thing for him in his state of exhaustion, but simply because it was more quickly procurable than anything else.

Of course we guessed something was wrong, and were burning with impatience to hear all, but we would not allow him to tell his story until he had eaten something, and even then it was difficult to connect his stammering sentences or form a distinct idea of what had occurred.

The fact was poor Magog had not a pleasant story to tell, and a very few words were sufficient for me! It seems they had all started the day before, really under the impression that nothing of importance would take place, and taking no provisions with them. They had presently become involved in an engagement, with (they said), about 6000 Gcalekas, and speedily succeeded in compelling the enemy to retire, killing several hundreds.

They were, however, rash enough to pursue the retreating foe, until they found, to their dismay, that the flight had been a *ruse de guerre*, and that they had now to encounter a host of warriors, (they said about 10,000 more), perfectly armed and fresh to the field, by whom they were completely surrounded.

A panic seems to have ensued,—the gun broke down somehow or other, and became disabled, and, feeling as the gallant 24th must have done on the fatal field of Isandlhana, that to remain was to be massacred, the little band, (not like the gallant 24th,) cut their way through—and—left. [1]

My heart seemed to cease beating as I listened with breathless interest to the short, disjointed sentences which proclaimed the tale of woe; sympathy, I could and did offer, but admiration I could neither feel nor express. Feeling, if men were going to retire from the field, women had better go to the front, I left the room to think over what had to be done.

One moment alone, to check the torrent of proud and passionate tears which would rise at the thought of my country's defeat; and now, with a heart that could feel no more, and nerves that seemed to have congealed into petrified iron, I returned; prepared to face the worst, and go quietly through whatever lay before me. I hardly realized the change that had passed over me, until I heard my own voice, cold and stern, and saw the start the two men gave as I re-entered the room.

"Oh! my missis, my dear missis," cried loving Johanna, "don't look at us like that; take a glass of wine, now do,—why you are

---

1. I do not vouch for the accuracy of this account of the Guadana fight. I am not writing a military history, but simply relating an Englishwoman's experiences during the war; so I merely attempt to supply the version which was told to me, and I have no reason to doubt that it is correct.

like a piece of hice."—The good soul amused me even then, and I was glad to hold her kind, warm hand while I inquired if the enemy were now in pursuit, and how soon they would be here?

"In about half an hour, I should think; they are coming to burn your house down tonight."

In half an hour!—why, half an hour must have passed already, I thought; how can those men sit there talking while there is so much to be done in these few precious moments?—I longed to get them out of the house, and suggested they should go over to Mr. Cumming's, and see what preparations were being made for defence. They now begged me to accompany them, kindly offering to carry the children over, as Mr. Cummings' house had a roof of corrugated iron, while mine could only boast one of thatch. I declined, feeling that if I had to die, I would die in my husband's home; and they departed, eager for news of any nature.

It was a great relief when they were gone, and Mrs. Gog and I now held a council of war; the good creature behaving nobly; never once reproaching me for having innocently brought her into so much trouble, and showing pluck and energy enough to have fitted out handsomely, a few dozen of the men now trembling and croaking about the reserve.

We now decided that if the worst came to the worst, she should try to escape with the children, and make their way down to the coast. Of course this was a chimerical idea, as we did not know that we were already completely cut off from the colony by a vast horde of foes. But a second suggestion was more sensible and practical; and upon it we acted at once.

Should the dreaded fire-stick be placed under our thatched roof; in a few minutes our store-room, containing paraffin oil, &c., would be burnt to the ground; and the valuable stock of provisions which my husband had purchased as a year's supply, would be entirely lost. The first thing to be done was to pack into something fireproof, a stock of provisions of the most compact and nourishing nature; such as tins of oatmeal, Swiss milk, chocolate, &c. Charmed to relieve our suspense with useful labour, we took a lamp and went out into the veranda. Fortunately the night was warmer than usual, and our excitement prevented our taking cold, as we were too hurried to wait for shawl or hat. We looked out a little cautiously, and I may be excused if I confess that my heart beat quicker when I stumbled over something living and warm, and felt something of the same kind touch my shoulder! A second glance showed that some sheep and cows had taken refuge on the *stoep*, and we gained the store-room safely. We got a tin box packed carefully and judiciously in a very short time, and did not forget to put in a case of lucifer-matches, some candles, and a few boxes of tinned fish and sardines. We also managed to cram in a ham and some pots of jam for the poor children; and the whole thing was quite a *multum in parvo* and presented almost a military air of neatness.

The gentlemen had now returned, and commending our work, carried the box to a safe place; where it would be concealed, and yet easily attainable in case of emergency. They informed us that several of the "heroes" had now returned, but that many were missing, having probably gone to Ibéka; and no one knew what had become of the "commander-in-chief." This aspect of affairs was not very charming, but as there must now have been upwards of sixty men in *laager* at the Idutywa, I naturally imagined they would decide to fortify and defend the place.

We now requested Magog and the other orderly to remain in our house during the night, to be at hand should anything occur; and though it was not likely they would be able to sleep much, went through the form of preparing "shake-downs "for them in the dining-room, as they might as well get as much rest as possible after their late terrible fatigues. When this was done, nurse and I retired, leaving the front door unlocked, so that the patrols could give us information without delay, and we then went to my room in which lay the sleeping children, utterly unconscious of the danger which surrounded them.

We thought it wisest to rest if possible, as we had nothing

more to do, and did not know what fatigue might await us; but I had scarcely donned my dressing-gown when a firm, manly tread came up the steps and along the passage, and I was informed that "Commandant" Allan Maclean wished to speak to me. I threw a shawl over my dressing gown and went to the dining-room, only too thankful to know there was someone at hand whose courage I could depend upon, and upon whose advice I could rely.

But what charmed me most was, that in that moment of danger and excitement, his whole mind and heart seemed occupied by his wife and his home, and I wished I could have told Mrs. Maclean how lovingly and kindly he spoke of her having sent him a "cake," which he was "going off to eat at once." He declined the supper which I offered, and I liked him all the better for declining, for I thought his wife's cake would be the sweetest *bonne-bouche* he could possibly have.—Now for business.—I knew Mr. Maclean had been appointed temporary commandant at Idutywa, and thought he might have come to say our house was required for military purposes, so smoothed the way by saying, our house and possessions were entirely subject to his commands in any way best adapted for the public service. At the same time I objected to leaving home, and going as a refugee to Mr. Cumming's, and asked if he considered this step necessary?

"Not at all," he replied; "you will be much more quiet and comfortable here. But tell me are you afraid?"

"Not in the least," I answered.

He seemed satisfied; and then promised that, come what might, I should be left undisturbed up to "the last ten minutes."—This happily arranged, my mind was more at rest; and after a few kind words to Mrs. Gog, who was quite a favourite with them all, the commandant departed, having cheered and encouraged us immensely.

That night, the 27th September, passed away;—I cannot say peacefully, but we did not encounter any of the predicted horrors,—nor was our house burnt down. It was impossible to sleep! Gentlemen seemed to be talking in the dining-room and

Bachelors' Den all night, and the front door was opened every five minutes. However, nurse and I rested a little, and took care of our poor babies, and felt more drawn to each other by this short time of suspense and peril, than by years of ordinary service or friendship.

CHAPTER 25

Off again

When Friday morning dawned we almost wished it were still night, for the effort to attend to the ordinary duties of the household seemed just the hardest thing of all to accomplish; and the brilliant sunshine seemed almost a mockery to the misery which surrounded us. But we had refugees to entertain, bread to bake, and a thousand other things to think of; so we braced ourselves with a cup of coffee, and were quite bright by breakfast time.

I superintended as usual, but my head was aching so much that I could not even take a cup of tea, and nothing but the early coffee passed my lips for many an hour after that. Our house was now like a barrack; people coming and going without a word of apology, and every feeling of ordinary etiquette seemed entirely set aside. I went to my bedroom, hoping for a little peace and quiet, but at that moment four officers—the two Mr. Macleans, Mr. Hamilton, and Mr. Cochrane—came to tell me the Gcalekas in overwhelming numbers were supposed to be the other side of the hill, and I must prepare to leave Idutywa in ten minutes.

"Can you be ready in that time?" they kindly inquired.

"Of course," I replied; "everything is ready now."

There was no time to ask what we were going to do, and I felt perfect confidence that they had arranged everything in the best way possible under the circumstances. I now went to nurse; told her to dress herself and the children instantly (their clothes had been put out in readiness previously), and send the Kafir servants to bid me farewell. I had paid their wages the day before, but the good girls had refused to leave me until the last moment, and now clung sobbing to my dress; kissing my hands, and even my feet, in their anxiety to express the sorrow and fidelity they could not put into words. I looked round hastily for some souvenir, and seeing two boxes of trinkets lying on the table, made the poor things smile through their tears by pouring the contents into the neat little aprons which both wore to please their "missis." I then threw a blanket over each girl's head, and sent them away laughing after all.

The interview with their mother was not so agreeable. The tiresome creature had, in defiance of my express commands, persisted in washing the huge bundle she had come for in the morning. The Kafirs are most irritating people in any case of emergency, as they persist in resisting every attempt at departure from ordinary routine, and will not move out of the accustomed groove for anything short of physical persuasion.

Even at this moment of anxiety and hurry, the old soul actually refused to bring the things, and harassed me by calmly sitting down to argue the matter while every second of time was precious; and we had to employ physical force before she could be induced to obey. A bundle of things, soaking wet, soon appeared; and was thrown down in the sun to dry. The newly-baked bread was taken from the oven, wrapped up in a cloth, and in less than ten minutes we were all ready. And now ensued a most trying time of suspense.

I did not know what plans had been formed, and as I was completely in the hands of others, had nothing to do but await instructions. I was rather surprised, when about half-an-hour passed away without any message coming for me, and still more astonished when, at the expiration of upwards of an hour, I found Mr. Maclean sitting on the doorstep, looking the picture of weariness, holding his head between his hands. I begged him to rest in the house, and inquired how it was nothing had yet been definitely settled.

At this moment Mr. Allan Maclean rode up and explained that everything was in a state of chaos and confusion; that the traders had not yet decided the knotty question as to whether Idutywa was to be abandoned or defended; that he could no longer wait, and must be off at once. He was in a great hurry, but was kind enough to cord some boxes for me even then; and dismounted again to pick up my little boy who had fallen down on the ground. So kind, so brave, so calm, so collected—he was quite one's ideal of a soldier, and I wished South Africa might possess many such sons to raise her standard and elevate her into a great and brave nation. The other brother soon left, and I then felt I had lost my best friends; for few others seemed to be capable of anything but to wander about, talking to, and terrifying everybody else.

When two hours had passed away, nurse and I began to resign ourselves to the idea that patience had better be cultivated, so we fed the children, and then sat down in the veranda to wait. I now saw Magog approaching, and seeing I must think for myself, decided upon a course of action. He told me the popular feeling was in favour of a flight *en masse* to Blythwood Seminary, a strongly-built mission house and station in the heart of Fingoland, (the country belonging to our allies).

Of course I opposed this idea, feeling our country had already lost prestige in the eyes of the natives, and that no effort or sacrifice was too great to recover it. Had my husband been there, I felt certain he would have decided to stay; and as his wife, it was my duty to remain. At the same time I felt my position keenly, for, in case I decided for the worst, what should I say to that husband, should his children perish?—I was now greatly gratified by finding that our escort were quite on my side, and willing to stand by me to the last.

I was much touched when they put their lives in my hands; saying they would abide by my decision, and obey my orders to the death, and that they left the responsibility entirely to me! So much fidelity; far more than I expected or deserved, was indeed a comfort in that time of trial; and I felt I must leave the matter in higher hands than mine, as the responsibility of their lives was too great. So I told them that if they could induce four other men to join them, making their number up to six, we would do our best to defend the Idutywa, though every other soul should leave it.

They went away, and for many weary hours did everything in their power to animate the crowd with courage, and induce them to remain. All in vain! every hour increased the difficulty; for the men, excited already by the danger of our situation, were fortifying themselves with "Dutch courage," and became less and less amenable to reason.—And now ensued a fearful scene, which I would fain forget.—Would that some other pen had undertaken the task of portraying the horrors of that dreadful day!

Nothing but the wish to bring before my countrymen and countrywomen a faithful picture of the state of things which existed in South Africa at that time would induce me to draw the veil, but I will spare my readers as much as I can, and beg them to imagine the rest for themselves.

Some men came up and asked me for the key of our store-room, pretending they were going to pack a supply of flour, sugar, and other provisions for my benefit, should I be compelled to share the flight. I was overcome with gratitude at this unexpected piece of consideration; and though my head was aching so violently that I could hardly speak or stand, I managed to walk to the store-room in order to thank them specially, and beg them to take what they pleased for themselves, after they had provided for me.

I thought their manner was very odd, when they laughed at each other in a curious way; but, putting it down to ignorance, quietly watched them helping themselves to sides of bacon, hams, &c., and dipping into the sugar and flour barrels with no measured hand. I need scarcely say that they must have misunderstood my instructions, as on my arrival at Blythwood I found myself a pauper; without so much as a crumb of bread to eat, while everyone around was eating ham, &c., without offering me any, or remembering that many had now a chance to assist one at whose table they had eaten many a meal.

But this was not the worst. They soon discovered some ale, which my husband had taken from the cellar to supply the house until his return; (most fortunately they did not discover the cellar itself, which was concealed under the floor of the dining-room.) And now I had to see my little home turned into a drinking-hall! Man after man arrived (nearly all strangers to me), to eat and drink at their will.

They spilt the gravy over my tablecloth and made a fearful noise, passing me on the *stoep* without a word of thanks, and soon the house was no place for a woman, and I was obliged to remain outside in the veranda, as the sun was blazing on the *veldt*. Much of this disorder was due to the fact of there being at that moment no magistrate at Idutywa, Mr. Cumming having been replaced by the commander of the corps of police, who had not yet arrived. There was no authority to appeal to, and I could only feel thankful I had the support of my brave and faithful white servant, who never left me for an instant, and did all she could to quell the uproar and keep the men in good humour.

I was now startled by the apparition of one of the refugees we had sheltered, who, in a very excited voice, exclaimed, "Mrs. Prichard, you are a coward! my mission is to heal wounds, not to make them; I have no quarrel with the Kafirs, they are great friends of mine; it is you who ought to make a stand against them."

I was too ill and weak to reply, but Mrs. Gog, who saw the man was not quite himself, pacified him, and gradually persuaded him to go away. This sort of thing—only getting worse and worse—actually went on until sunset, when Magog came to say it was simply impossible to get another man to join in the defence, and that, as a friend, he advised my joining the party who were now really going to start for Blythwood, after wasting all the invaluable hours of daylight in gossip, groans, and talk! He told me that, as my husband had taken away the government wagon, and we had no carriage of our own, a very gentlemanly trader, a Mr. C—— F—— , had kindly promised to take the elder child and myself in his buggy (an open sort of gig), and that another gentleman had been good enough to consent to take charge of the nurse and baby, who would travel in his wife's wagon.

The idea of separation from my baby and faithful nurse at such a crisis almost stunned me with horror, but I could not dictate, and had to submit; physical pain and long fasting having diminished my powers of resistance. They reassured me by saying the wagons ought to arrive at Blythwood "tomorrow at latest," and added, that they would be protected by a force of police, and be far safer than we should. Magog now conducted me to the other house, which I found in a state of confusion, greater if possible than our own.—Men were arming and gesticulating, women weeping and children crying, and the place was completely changed.—I gathered a tiny rose, the only sweet thing in that sad scene, and took it away as a souvenir of Idutywa, giving one look at the home I should never see again. And now I must bid *adieu* to good Johanna, and kiss my baby for perhaps the last time.

"May Heaven protect you till we meet again," was all I could whisper; and in another moment I was seated in the buggy, with little Henry on my lap, and we had dashed off at a fearful pace. We were preceded by a mule wagon conveying Mrs. Cumming and her children, and followed by the escort and several other gentlemen on horseback (among whom was Mr. Budge, nurse's sweetheart), all armed to the teeth and fine, strong men. The horses were very fresh, spirited creatures, and required all Mr. F——'s skill and strength to hold them in.

We soon left the main road and dashed, "over hill, over dale," at a terrible pace. The sun went down, and now a bitter wind arose which soon blew away my hat. I longed to throw a shawl over my head, but had not a hand to spare or a moment to lose, for we were driving for our lives; it was a race with the Foe, and the prize was Life! The carriage swayed to and fro; the seat was uncomfortably high, and it was almost more than I could do at times to hold the child upon my lap.

Not a word was exchanged for miles; our kind charioteer had enough occupation for head and hands! The day before he was a rich man, and was actually on his way down to the colony, intending to retire from business, having made a comfortable fortune, when he heard that his store and stock had been entirely destroyed.

"Fifty pounds in the world, and the coat on my back!" he laughed at me; "but I know my wife and little girl are safe at Queenstown by this time, so we must just climb up the hill again; that's all!"

Nothing could exceed his kindness and consideration for my position, and he tried to put me at my ease by reminding me of some very small act of courtesy on our part a few days before, which I had completely forgotten, and which did not deserve a single word of thanks.

And now we find that we have got separated from the rest of the party, as they find it impossible to keep up at the furious rate we are going; and for one second we halt, and glance around. We were apparently alone; on the top of grassy hills which stretched for miles in every direction, and without a tree or a rock by way of a beacon;—we seemed to have got on to the tip top of the world, and the very vultures soared below us. But look! quick! we are far from being alone!—on the contrary, we are surrounded by a group of armed Kafirs in their native war-paint and paraphernalia; armed to the teeth, and determined to arrest our progress. They stop the horses, who try to dash through, and foam and fret at this delay; and their excited gestures, fierce voices, and angry language, tell us to prepare for the worst. My new friend gives me one look;—pale as death, but quiet and composed; he never loses command of the reins, and mutters hoarsely,

"I'm afraid we have no chance; can you understand what they say?"

I shake my head sadly in reply, and crush down my child under my dress, to hide him from the crowd of warriors who now push their hands into the carriage, and ever press, closer and closer, as if they wished to crush us to death.—What is this mesmeric influence which is stealing over me?—I begin to feel a strange fascination in watching the ever-closing circle of hideous and fantastic figures around me! How many minutes will it be before that man pierces my heart with the *assegai* which seems already pointed towards me?

All sense of fear or dread of suffering is mercifully spared me, and I am only aware of the nervous sensation one goes through during the detestable process of being photographed, or the equally uncomfortable effort of waiting for a gun to be fired. Mechanically I begin to count, *sotto voce*, one two three—oh, for heaven's sake, put us quickly out of our misery!—when the rapid gallop of horses' feet is heard; and on the arrival of our own armed escort, the Kafirs fall back.—We shall never know whether they were Friends or Foes; they did not look very affectionately at us, and only allowed us to proceed after they had been favoured with a very rose-coloured version of the Guadana affair, which was, we thought, excusable under the circumstances.

A hurried entreaty to our friends to keep up if they could at any price, and away we dash, but, alas! only to lose our way in every direction; and by midnight we are in pitch darkness, and have no idea how near we are to the enemy. Crash, crunch! and the horses' heels are almost on our faces, while we are all hurled violently forward; for the carriage has dashed over into a ravine—a bed of a river—something or other very steep, and a shriek rises from poor, little Henry's hitherto uncomplaining lips.

"Can you manage to crawl out? I am afraid I can't help you; the horses are so restive, and I can see there's no water in the *sluit*?"

"Oh! yes. I am all right; no bones broken," I reply, and scramble out; feeling first a rock and then some sand, on which I lie on my face, while I feel for the poor child, and drag him out by the heels. He is as good as possible, and leans patiently against my shoulder, while we sit upon a stone and try to see where we are. But now the gentlemen ride up; and some dismount and come to our assistance, while the others look after their horses.

Some kind soul drags me up a bank, saying in tones a mother might use to her child, "You can never know how sorry we all are for you, Mrs. Prichard." Another good man carries my boy, and in a few minutes we find we are in close proximity to a Kafir *kraal*; but whether belonging to Friends or Foes, we know not. The gentlemen now attempt to mend the carriage, and as this promises to be a long business, I drag my weary, shaken limbs, slowly crawling along the grass; until I reach the gentlemen, to whisper a request for the carriage cushions and some wraps.

These being promptly brought, I make a comfortable bed "on the *veldt*," and, wrapping my child in a warm shawl, lie down by his side to rest.—That quiet time under the stars, was the first peaceful moment I had enjoyed for days; and the sweet influence of the sleeping child, who lay so tranquilly in my arms, soothed and strengthened my shaken nerves.—The blue sky above was the loveliest of canopies, and the bright stars twinkled and spar-kled away so merrily that they were most cheerful company.

Under such influences, who could think much of the war-cloud's around us, or wish to remain long away from that realm of peace and love?—This was the poetical side of the affair; the prose version was not so agreeable! The night air, (winter time, remember; 3000 feet above the sea,) was bitterly cold; and though I had now enveloped my head in a shawl, my chest was very sore, and I was rapidly losing the small remnant of voice which was left me after the vocal fatigues of the day.

I was burning with fever and shivering from cold at one and the same time, and wondered absently what would happen if I were to have a serious illness, and who would take care of the children. These meditations were interrupted by one of the gentlemen, who came to tell me they had found out where we were.—That we were safe in Fingoland, but that, as it would be impossible to reach Blythwood that night, we should content ourselves by trying to get to a trader's shop, which could not be more than three miles away.

Greatly cheered by this good news, I gladly returned to the carriage, and with some difficulty, but without any adventure, we gradually arrived at our destination.

The good folks there were speedily aroused, and, instead of displaying annoyance at our intrusion, greeted us in the very kindest way, taking in the whole of our large party for the night. The shop belonged to some Mr. Allan, but there seemed to be two brothers;—I remember it all like a dream, and should not know their faces, I fear, if I saw them again, but their hospitality and warm welcome I can never forget; and I write these pages in the earnest hope that they may chance to see them and learn that I really did appreciate their goodness to us.

They led us through an enormous store into a little back room, with a deal table in the centre, and settles of the back-woods' order by way of chairs.—We had not been one moment in the room, before Mrs. Cumming's children and my little boy were playing "wolf" under the table as naturally as if they had lived in the house all their lives, and were accustomed to sitting up until two in the morning every day!

Mr. Allan now laid (I was going to say, the cloth, but I should say) the table, for supper; bringing bread, biscuits, butter, and his last pot of raspberry jam for the children; and, to our great joy, boiling the kettle and making a huge jorum of tea. The children much appreciated these luxuries, and ate ravenously, poor little dears! but we grownups were too sick at heart to swallow a mouthful, though all made the effort in order to please our kind young hosts.

The tea was, however, an unspeakable comfort, and we were more grateful for this impromptu meal than many a guest is for a Lord Mayor's dinner! After supper Mr. Allan showed us another room in which the ladies and children were to sleep, and provided us with lovely new blankets out of the shop, to convert into mattresses and coverlets. The gentlemen had to rest upon the long counter in the store, but I fear they did not sleep much; nor could we ladies do anything but talk. The children, however, were soon asleep, and seemed to think the whole affair a most charming picnic, and that it was excessively grand to go to bed with their clothes on.

I stopped talking at last from sheer want of voice, and fell into a doze, which lasted until daybreak. About five a.m. Magog brought us some nice, hot cocoa, and told us to get up at once as we were to start immediately. I tried to reply, but found my voice had completely vanished, and I could not even whisper in anything approaching to a lady-like manner. I also felt as if every limb had been upon the rack, and was altogether so cramped and feverish and miserable, that it was difficult even to summon the "nods and becks and wreathed smiles," that had to do duty for words. We were soon ready; our kind hosts insisting upon our sitting down to breakfast before we started, and evidently quite distressed because we did such scanty justice to their good fare.

CHAPTER 26

Arrival of the Wagons

We started about seven o'clock, and at first the air was very cold; but soon the delicious sunshine appeared to gladden our hearts and cheer us on our way. Of course my mental thermometer rose at least fifty degrees at once, and I was soon enjoying the very beautiful hill-scenery by which we were on all sides surrounded. There were several little streams to cross, and it was pleasant to descend from the buggy and go over the stepping-stones, and I should really have enjoyed the whole thing very much had I not begun to feel excessively nervous about our reception at Blythwood, and I sincerely wished it could still have been my lot to have remained in my home and be in a position to offer, instead of ask for, shelter and hospitality.

I now remembered that the handsome, Scotch lassie, who had been my sister-passenger in the *European*, from Cape Town to East London, had told me she was going to keep house for her elder brother, at a mission station called "Blythwood," and it flashed upon me that possibly this nice little lady might be the Miss Macdonald whose name was now on every lip, for was she not to be our hostess?

On inquiry I found this to be the case, and the reflection comforted me somewhat, as it was far pleasanter than to have to encounter a perfect stranger. I also hoped that the wagons would bring my little stock of "rations" during the afternoon, so that I might not have to ask for more than one meal.—Occupied by these reflections, I did not notice the scenery until we suddenly descended a hill, and saw before us a small river, on the opposite side of which rose the handsome stone building which Mr. F—— informed me was the Kafir College at Blythwood.

I was not prepared to find such an imposing edifice in that lonely land, and was glad to see it was so strongly built and well constructed; we could quite imagine its being converted into an impromptu fortress at once in case of emergency. I beheld a very long, stone building, with a lofty entrance in the centre, and two rows of windows, which pierced the building on either side. Above this was another row, which extended without intermission in one unbroken line, and the whole effect was good and enduring.

At the present moment the appearance was somewhat marred by the fact that the edifice was not quite completed, and it was also disfigured by the wooden barricades which protected every window in front of the house. Magog now rode on to prepare the principal for our arrival, and returned with the good news that Mrs. Eustace (wife of Colonel Eustace) was there already, and was ready to greet me in the kindest way; while little Miss Macdonald seemed quite pleased at the thought of meeting again, and recalling our pleasant voyage in the *European*.

My kind new acquaintance, Mr. F——, now surrendered his charge into the hands of others, and I greatly deplored the loss of voice which prevented my thanking him as I wished. I can only say, his great courtesy and kindness will never be forgotten either by my husband or myself, and no one rejoiced more than we when we heard that his energy had retrieved his broken fortunes, and that he was again a successful man.—Magog now took me into the house and presented me to Mrs. Eustace, whose charming manner, and bright, cheerful expression won my heart at once; her bewitchingly sweet and clear voice was giving me the most delightful of welcomes, and I felt I was indeed fortunate to have such a thorough lady, in every best sense of the word, in the house.

Mrs. Eustace now led me into the large room, which had been temporarily converted into a reception-room for the women and children who were arriving from all parts of the country; some in a state of destitution equal to my own. She then startled me with the inquiry, if I would like some breakfast? Breakfast! I thought it was dinner-time.

The fact was, we had gone through so much already that day, that the time had passed slowly, and I was surprised to find it was only about nine o'clock in the morning. Mrs. Eustace skimmed away to the kitchen and soon brought back some tea and bread and butter, which Henry and I much enjoyed. It was the first solid food I had taken for nearly forty hours, but I could cot swallow much, as my throat was very painful. Mrs. Eustace seemed quite at home already, and infused—or did her best to infuse—brightness and courage in every direction.

Some, however, refused to be comforted, and soon the two sets divided, the melancholy mortals being left to weep at will on one side of the room, while those who joined Mrs. Eustace's "band of hope" preferred the sunny side, and clustered about, laughing over our various adventures, and relating the experiences which had befallen us all during the two previous days, (27th and 28th of September).

Mr. Macdonald, the principal, now entered the room, and was greeted with smiles on his right hand and by tears and sighs on his left. He seemed to prefer sunshine to cloud, for, on apportioning to each lady her apartment and position in the house, we found, to our amusement, that smiles had the best of it, and dear Mrs. Eustace at once took possession of the very large room, at that moment used as a drawing-room , while a most charming apartment at the end of the corridor was allotted to me.

I rather pitied Mr. Macdonald, for his position was somewhat trying; rival claims appeared on every hand, and he must have known that, however he decided, he must annoy some. He did not, however, allow himself to be influenced or disturbed in any way, and having quietly but firmly made his own arrangements, went upstairs to divide the vacant space there among the families of the trading class who crowded every yard of available space.

Our discomforts and trials were as nothing in comparison to theirs. Only a small portion of the upper story had been yet partitioned into rooms, as the building was not finished, and the poor women had to put up shawls, &c., to ensure privacy. People were crowded closely, and it was impossible to put less than two or three families into one room.

The staircase was not yet made, and they had to come and go by means of a ladder, up and down which poor neglected children scrambled all day, while their overwrought mothers, baby in arms, vainly endeavoured to attend to everything at once, and to carry on the ordinary avocations of life without the most ordinary appliances!

No one had ventured to add their servants to the list of claimants for houseroom and hospitality, so we all had to do everything as best we could, and turn one's hand to whatever was most needed. I, however, had nothing to cook; and as Mrs. Eustace had kindly invited me to share the leg of mutton she was fortunate enough to have obtained for that day's dinner, I confined my labours to arranging my room, dusting the furniture kindly lent for my use by Miss Macdonald, and sweeping the floor with the one long broom Miss Macdonald supplied to the ladies; other appliances had, of course, also to be used in turn, and this wasted a great deal of time and caused some unavoidable annoyance. Magog and the other policeman, whom I will call "Mr. Bird," were most kind in assisting me; bringing water from the river, amusing Henry, and telling me they had lighted a campfire on the *veldt* on which they had cooked something, (their rations, I suppose,) which they vainly implored me to eat.

I now found to my horror that I was rapidly becoming very ill, and the effort of using the long broom was much greater than I had expected. I found, too, that one requires practice even to sweep a floor properly, and my first performance was not exactly the success I had confidently expected it would be! However, I "went at it" again after dinner, and got on so much better that I looked forward to surprising Mrs. Gog by the announcement that I was independent of her services so far as housework was concerned!

Little Miss Macdonald brought me some tea and sandwiches with her own hands, and I should have been entirely comfortable had I not been harassed by the thought that I was consuming food which could ill be spared by those who so generously supplied it, and weighed down with heavy anxiety at the non-arrival of the wagons, especially as I saw this anxiety reflected in the countenances of everyone else. I now had another trial which, for the time, banished other painful thoughts; my little boy became feverish and slightly delirious, and was seized with an attack of croup. I had nothing whatever at hand to relieve him except cold water, which he drank eagerly, and at last his struggles and delirium obliged me to summon Magog to my assistance, as I could no longer control the child.

I now found the gentle giant the kindest and tenderest of nurses. He soothed and composed the little invalid, actually undressed him with his own hands (as the poor child had taken a feverish dislike to me, and would not allow me to touch him) and put him to bed; not leaving until all danger was over, and the poor, little refugee was forgetting the excitement of the previous day in refreshing sleep. I now lay down myself, as I had no candles and no matches, but I was very ill all night, and when a gentle tap was heard at the door next morning, could hardly summon sufficient strength to open it.—Outside stood a lady with a sheet of paper, an envelope, pen, and a miniature bottle of ink in her hand; she told me the post was going at once, and would I like to write to my friends in England, (evidently thinking my husband was no more) to say where I was?—I must write very few words, as we must be careful with the ink, and the pen was wanted by somebody else!

I stood by the mantelpiece and scribbled a few lines to my mother, but violent shivering fits now came on, and I threw myself on the bed, just as I was, in my dress and jacket, little thinking three days and nights would pass before I rose again. I was practically speechless, in agonies of pain, and almost fainting with weakness and utter collapse of the system. Some kind lady soon discovered my plight, and all came in the most unselfish way to my assistance!

Pretty Miss Gilbert (who had visited us at Idutywa), dressed and took care of Henry; swept and dusted my room, and did everything in the gentle, sweet way which made her so loveable and winning! Bonnie Miss Macdonald brought me tray after tray of the most temptingly-arranged food, and was deeply distressed at my lack of appetite, while, Mrs. Eustace—was—Mrs. Eustace! I can offer her no higher praise! It was perhaps fortunate that I could not eat much, for we were now beginning to be terribly short of provisions.

Some of the police now volunteered to go to Mr. Barnett's and try to bring over a wagon of provisions to be divided between four ladies, of whom I was one. They did succeed, and brought back safely some barrels of flour and sugar, also some tea, and a few other things, and the traders upstairs consented to sell us Swiss milk and other things of that kind, at exorbitant prices, and after a good deal of persuasion. Their creed seemed to be of a nature so exquisitely plain and simple, that it was entirely comprised in the maxim that *Charity begins at home*. They therefore made up their minds not to sell until prices rose to the highest pitch, and one old lady who refused to sell me even a quarter of a pound of tea for ten shillings, declined my entreaties with the quiet reply, "No, my dear, the time will come when you will offer me five and twenty shillings for the quarter pound."

She had six or seven large chests at her side as she spoke, and would not let me have a single ounce, though she knew how much my health required it. [1] One could hardly expect the Kafirs to sell us meat or poultry while white people set such an example of greed and selfishness; so it was only very rarely that the wives and children of the officials tasted meat, though probably the traders' wives upstairs could tell a different story.

But to return; thus passed away three terrible days and nights,

---

1. This happened some time afterwards.

and all this time no trace of my baby! no news of nurse! I was almost frantic with suspense, and the impossibility of expressing my feelings in words, and the physical pain which pre- vented any exertion, made the hours doubly long. I never once slept for a single moment, and listened to every sound of approaching wheels or footsteps, with an agony only those who have gone through similar suffering can realize.

People around seemed to think I was unconscious, and the whispered words I heard exchanged about the missing wagon-party were only too sad a confirmation of my own fears. At last! one evening after ten o'clock, just after dear Mrs. Eustace had paid her final visit for the night, I heard a commotion in the corridor; and the glad cry, "The wagons have arrived!" flew from one end of the building to the other.

Animated and alive again, I sat up for the first time, and in the joy of feeling nurse's loving arms about me, and the rapture with which I looked on the darling she laid beside me, my voice returned, and with it a deluge of tears (the first I had shed), which probably saved me from severe illness.

"He's all right, dear; he's been as good as gold the 'ole journey, and lor! you should have see 'ow much notice he took of heverything! He's as warm as a toast—look!—I 'jumped' your pink dressing-gown to wrap him in, and it's as black as smuts with dust;—I hope you won't be vexed, mum!"

"Vexed!"—I threw my arms round her, and gave her a kiss for a reply; and now she turns to curtsey to Mrs. Eustace, who comes in to say she is "making some coffee for nurse, and will she be kind enough to come and take it, after she has finished her chat with her mistress?"

"What a lady!" utters Johanna in tones of gratitude as she leaves, quite appreciating the kind thoughtfulness as much, as I did.

Nurse departs, and in walk several police (apparently thinking war makes everything *en règle*), carrying certain boxes and bundles of clothing, blankets—and—yes! the box of provisions which Johanna and I packed last Thursday night.

Dear little *multum in parvo*! What a treasure you will be to us now! But here comes nurse,—bustles the men out of the room, and sends them off laughing for more bundles, until I begin to think the room will never hold the things.

"Lor, mum! what a place for you to be in, and what a mess they have made of your floor!" (so she didn't appreciate my broom after all); "but never mind, I've got a beautiful box of soap in the wagon, and I'll put you all to rights in the morning."

I now began to wonder where nurse was going to sleep; there was only a rather small bed in the room, and with all my respect for nurse, the idea of sharing that necessary article of furniture with her was anything but an agreeable prospect! Still, I could not put that kind soul on the floor, after all her devotion to baby; so we actually slept four in a bed (and this continued for many, many weeks), by dint of lying across the broad side instead of the usual lengthway of the bed. I took good care to use the two children as "buffers," but there was no chance of forgetting my lady-companion, and this apparently trifling annoyance was a greater trial to me than any other hardship!

However, I was glad enough to get Johanna back at any price, and slept soundly for the first time that week.

CHAPTER, 27

A Visit from my Husband

When I awoke I was startled to see a bright fire blazing on the hearth (the grates were not yet put in), in such close proximity to the bed that it was quite dangerous. "Just you lie still, mum, and drink your tea; nobody wants you to get up. You just leave everything to old Johanna, and get well; that's your business."

Ah, how I enjoyed every drop of that tea, my own too, and I could not resist one little feeling of triumph at the thought I had not paid exorbitantly for it, which gave the finishing touch to my satisfaction! And now I see Johanna frizzling away at something in a saucepan, which is evidently mutton and bacon (by way of a fancy-dish, I suppose).

I dislike mutton in the morning at any time, and must inquire into the extravagance of cooking twice as much as we shall require, when we must hoard every crumb of food. "Well, mum, you can't call me extravagant," replies the aggrieved *cuisinière*, "for the bacon is your own, mum, and the mutton is off a beautiful leg, which Mr, Budge"—(a giggle and a sigh)—"give me this morning."

"Oh, you wicked woman! so that is why you are so anxious I should get up late in the morning, is it? Very well, Johanna, you and I will have a race tomorrow, and if Mr. Budge ventures to appear round the corner, I shall shoot him with the broomstick.—No,—on second thoughts, pray give my compliments to Mr. Budge, and tell him, I am most grateful and the leg is delicious. But Johanna, I am not an Arab lady; do you expect me to eat meat—bacon especially—with my fingers?"

"My dear, I've been all over the house to borrow some forks, but they're all in use, and I could only get one spoon and a knife."

"Never mind; I am fond of sandwiches, and the bread is so stale" (baked nearly a week ago) "that I can manage capitally."

After breakfast, I get up and dress, and imagine I am going to do wonders in the way of unpacking and arranging the room, but, to my dismay, find I can hardly stand, and feel just as if I had had a very long illness. I am on the point of lying down again to rest, when I catch sight of something most repulsive in a corner. Johanna insists that it is all right and can't be helped, but I also insist, and she now tells me it is dried manure which we shall have to convert into fuel, for there is nothing else to use for the fires, as the Kafirs will not venture from home to cut or sell wood (of which also, there is a scarcity)! The whole thing is so utterly horrible, that I can but bear it silently, and comfort myself with the reflection that I am no worse off than others. It has to be borne, and there is an end of it.

By dint of resting and working alternately, I contrive to get the room into something like order that day, and by next morning begin regular routine. We rise at five a.m. and dress before the children awake; make their toilets; and at six a.m. I take baby in my arms and go out to sit in the fresh air with the children until nine o'clock, when we return to breakfast. Meanwhile nurse has scrubbed the floor (an operation performed daily), prepared breakfast and laid the table, having also tidied the room and made the bed.

We hire a Kafir woman to wash for us, but imagine she does not understand the art of getting-up linen, so after breakfast nurse goes away to starch and iron, bake bread and cook what dinner we can get. Things begin to look more comfortable, as I have unpacked our own house-linen and silver, and we no longer have to use our fingers, _à la mode de Paradis_. Mr. Macdonald has also vacated the kitchen for the benefit of the officials' wives, using the fire in the great hall for his own cuisine, so that we are not obliged to have the fire or fuel in our room, which is a blessing!

Our furniture is somewhat scanty, but we use a box for a table, and sit upon a bag of linen by way of a chair, and as there are no pillows or *bureaux*, we stuff pillow-cases full of children's clothes, &c., and thus combine both advantages in one.[1]

The weather also is simply superb and the morning air is doing the children and myself so much good; only,—I wish it would not make us quite so hungry!

The ground in front of the house is now occupied by a police camp, and the patrol tents make the place picturesque;—at the rear of the building a party of volunteers is constantly engaged in making an earthwork fortification, consisting of a deep trench and a high bank.

To the west is a *laager* of traders' wagons and camp fires, (for all cannot be accommodated within the building) and south and east we are protected by a boundary provided by nature; the pretty river which supplies us with water, but which, alas! the oxen are perceptibly diminishing in volume. As all the linen is washed in this stream, I should not be sorry to have a filter! There are no trees near enough to shade us in our morning walks, so the children and I encamp in the trenches to get the benefit of shade from the bank. I sit on an old tin bucket turned upside down. Baby sleeps on my lap, and Henry runs off and plays at "soldiers."

Meanwhile I get no news of my husband, until one day a Kafir knocks at the door, and tells me he has a letter for me from Captain Fraser. Wondering what this gentleman can have to write to me about, I open the note, which is a kind, little scribble on the leaf of a pocket-book; and find it contains the joyful information that he has just met my husband somewhere, told him where we are, (none of my letters had reached him,) and that I may hope to see Edward in a few days. I cannot thank our friend for his kindness, as his man has gone, but I do so now

---

1. I am particularly proud of this idea, and take the liberty of suggesting it to any readers placed in circumstances of the "*difficile*" order.

with all my heart.

On the 5th October I receive a flying visit from the aforesaid husband, who has many adventures of his own to relate, which may be appended to this volume, should another edition be published. He is horrified at my holding baby for three hours at a time before breakfast, as I also have the care of the children the entire morning until dinnertime, as nurse is supposed to be busy in the far-distant kitchen.

As Mrs. Nurse thinks it necessary to make an elaborate toilette every afternoon, which occupies an hour at least, after another hour occupied in washing up the very scanty amount of china and glass we have used at dinner, it may readily be imagined that I am not "off duty "until about five p.m., when she goes out for a walk with the children, and I begin my needlework, unless the room requires a second tidying, or I am so utterly exhausted that I have to lie down for a quiet half-hour.

This is the time at which Mrs. Eustace and I manage occasionally to exchange a few words to cheer and rest each other. Now the children return, and I am nurse again, while Johanna prepares tea. Then come the children's baths, and it is again eight p.m. before Mrs. Gog and I sit down to our needlework. I am making a grey dress, for most of my things are too good for this kind of work, and must be put away for brighter days.

All finery, too, seems so heartless and unsuitable at such a time, and Mrs. Eustace and I are anxious to protest by silent example, against the showy costumes which we see on all sides; some of the traders' wives apparently regarding the occasion as an opportunity of airing their best dresses, and appearing in the fashions seen in the last *Myra* or *Queen*, exaggerated to their utmost folly.

It is only the second gown I have ever attempted to make, and I am too nervous to blunder over it before clever nurse; so I mend things for the children until she goes to bed, and then sit up until one or two in the morning at my dressmaking. I then tumble into bed, and, like the celebrated Connaught Ranger, find, when I wake, "it is time to get up." My husband refuses to believe it necessary for Mrs. Gog to spend quite so much time in the kitchen, and administers a reprimand which brings a cloud upon the horizon. He also insists upon my hiring a Kafir girl to come very early every morning, and assist with, the children until sunset; and leaves me money, which I greatly need.

Edward further promises to go home next day, and ascertain what state the house is in, and says he will look for a missing box of baby-linen which has not yet turned up. (It got taken away by mistake on an ammunition-wagon to the military camp at Ibéka, and was eventually discovered at Komgha, the frontier town in the colony, the other side of the great Kei River, and was returned to me by a bachelor magistrate ten months afterwards!)

CHAPTER 28

"All's Well that ends Well"

I now begin to find it is the petty trials of war which are the hardest to bear. It had been pleasant enough to act the "Lady Bountiful" to a circle of refugees during a few days of excitement, with a chorus always at hand to applaud every action, word, and look. I now discovered the time had come to exercise the more feminine qualities of gentleness, patience, self-denial, and tact, which were called upon at every moment of each unexciting day, and which were tried in every possible way.

The incessant noise of the establishment was also a fearful strain upon one's nerves. The publicity of the life, the incessant confinement to one small room, and the association with persons of every class and type, were all equally trying, and the absence of letters, papers, or information of any kind, made the monotonous round of insignificant duties appear very irksome at times.

And now our provisions begin to fail, and we see *mealies*-(not the delicious, "green *mealies*," but the corn they feed the horses upon)—appearing at our repasts, and the said repasts are sometimes omitted altogether, according to circumstances! Insufficient nourishment makes us feel weak and irritable, and we become less fitted to do our duty, and less cheerful about our hardships. Our husbands and brothers are all away, (I refer to the ladies in the lower east corridor,) and we are harassed with anxiety about them.

One morning Mrs. Eustace comes to me with a pencilled

scrap written by the colonel on the field of Quintana. "Poor Mrs. Goss! "(upstairs, you know); "her husband and brother are killed! who can break the news to her? Oh, Mrs. Prichard, what if it is our turn next?"

I turn white with horror, and silently clasp her cold hand with a feeling of sister sympathy that requires no words to express its meaning!

And now we began to be greatly annoyed by the conduct of certain characters in *laager*, and it was hardly agreeable for ladies to leave the house at all, while the noise over our head at night became perfectly unbearable. On the 9th November, Captain Dearie, of the Port Elizabeth Volunteers, came over from Toleni with full authority to request these individuals to retire, which they accordingly did, to our unspeakable relief and joy!

Captain Dearie was accompanied by my husband, who was pushing on his work at Toleni as fast as possible, but was greatly hindered by the difficulty of getting the natives to work either regularly or steadily during these troublous times. Often, too, just as he had succeeded in getting together a tolerably good gang, a message would arrive from some magistrate ordering the men to go at once and join some levy he was raising; so it was rather slow work.

After a few weeks, however, the first grand excitement abated, and brave Mrs. Eustace was fortunate enough, to have the loan of a wagon offered to her, and succeeded in crossing the Kei, and arriving safely in the colony. A week later, and this gallant feat would have been impossible, for now a second and more dangerous rising of the Gcaikas again cuts off all communication with the colony, and we are virtually prisoners, and in a state of siege. Oh, how my heart ached as my dear friend drove away, and how I longed to accompany her; but duty must be done!

(My husband's work is of some importance to the public service at the present crisis, and he must push it on as rapidly as possible to facilitate transport and the movements of troops. He shall never say that his wife asked him to leave his post, and of course I will remain until every soldier has left the frontier, and my husband is at liberty to think of family considerations first.) Several other families took advantage of this lull in the storm to return to homes in the neighbourhood, and for the first time Blythwood became comparatively quiet. Mr. Macdonald and his sister took advantage of the opportunity to get down to the coast; but, before leaving, they were kind enough to give me the use of an additional room, next to my original one, begging me, in the kindest way, to remain at Blythwood "six months more, if I wish to do so."

We had not felt we could offer pecuniary remuneration for the room I had occupied, but my husband had had the pleasure of contributing to the funds of the institution, and paid, of course, for my board, during a few days in which I had been guest of Miss Macdonald. This had been during an interregnum in which I was without proper servants.

Very painful circumstances had made the dismissal of Mrs. Gog an imperative necessity before her six months were up, and we had not yet engaged the Kafir servants who took her place. I was sorry to be compelled to part suddenly from one to whom I was so much attached, but few ladies will wonder that, after the exciting nature of the scenes through which we had passed, and the close quarters in which, we now found ourselves, it was simply impossible to maintain the proper balance of relative position that should exist between mistress and maid.

Our present situation was also just of the nature to bring out the dark, rather than the bright side of her nature, and the fact of her engagement to a wealthy trader made anything like obedience utterly distasteful to her. She married Mr. Budge as soon as the war was over, and I wish them both every happiness, remembering only her faithful service in time of trouble, and preferring to forget the rather uncomfortable events which occurred at Blythwood.

I am also very thankful to have been compelled to dismiss her, as I might otherwise never have known how well one can get on with Kafir servants; I should have felt dependent upon the services of any white domestic, and afraid to reprove her

lest I might be left to their mercy. Of course there was some
trouble the first few days, but at any rate, one had the satisfaction
of knowing one's directions would be faithfully, if imperfectly,
fulfilled; and before a week was over we had no cause to regret
the change.

We now managed better about provisions, as my husband
was able to send a pack-horse, under the charge of escort, once
a week to Blythwood, and with the exception of butcher's meat,
which was still only occasionally to be obtained, I did pretty well,
and whenever we ran short, we fell back upon *mealies*. I was also
looking forward to a visit from Edward, who had promised to
spend Christmas with us, and he had sent over all the furniture,
china, glass, &c., saved from the wreck at Idutywa; so our rooms
began to look almost pretty, and I felt much more at home.

But there is no rose without a thorn, and one now appeared,
of insignificant dimensions, but very prickly and harassing. Mr.
Macdonald having gone, the entire command of the institution
was left in the hands of a carpenter. I will not quote the well-
known proverb about *Jack in Office*, and think there was every
excuse for the poor man, whose sudden elevation naturally bewildered and turned his head. (I should here mention that just
before the departure of Miss Macdonald, it had occurred to me
that we might possibly be allowed to take our meals in the room
left vacant by Mrs. Eustace, and sit there in the afternoon, as
it was now the height of summer, and the South African sun
blazed into both our rooms on the opposite side of the west
corridor for a very considerable portion of the day.)

I merely intended to bring over a table and our glass and
china, and was quite prepared to vacate at half an hour's notice,
should the room be required at any time. Miss Macdonald saw
no objection to this, and consented in the kindest way; the great
Mr. B. also approved, and everything went on smoothly for some
days. I had been most civil to the worthy carpenter, and little
foresaw the amusing feud which would ensue upon my modest
request. One day, however, I got a hint from a servant that Mr.
B. wanted to have that room (by far the largest and handsom-

est in the corridor) for the use of his wife and family! Naturally shrinking from the close association that would ensue, and above all, dreading contact with his children, I mentioned the hint to my husband, and, on his next visit, he was good enough to pay the carpenter the compliment of calling upon him at the very neat cottage in which he then resided.

My husband explained that it was a great convenience to me to have the use of the room, and requested that, if the authorities did not really require "Mrs. Eustace's room" for a few weeks longer, he should feel greatly indebted if I might remain. My husband returned, saying B. was quite amiable, and that I should not be disturbed. At this moment the carpenter approached, and I saw by his knitted brow, downcast bearing, and sulky countenance, that something was wrong; and with a woman's instinct said to my husband, "You are mistaken; I shall be insulted before you are five minutes' ride from Blythwood."

My husband laughed and left, and as he disappeared over the brow of the hill, a note was handed to me couched in most fiery terms; telling me that he—(the great B.)—would come "himself" and turn me out by main force if I had not cleared out by midday!

I need scarcely say that I did not send a written reply to this elegant *billet-doux*, but, wishing to avoid a scene, and knowing *Jack in office* really could turn me out if he chose, I slept over it, and in the morning sent a verbal message, ignoring the letter, and requesting Mr. B. "to be kind enough to come and speak to me, when he could conveniently do so."

I sat down quietly to my needlework to await his arrival, and as I quite excused the poor man's conduct on account of his ignorance, was indeed astonished when the door was suddenly thrown open, and Mr. B., white and trembling with rage, throwing his arms passionately above his head, and accompanied by several Kafir youths, rushed into the room, exclaiming; "I won't hear a word; it's no use you're speaking, for I won't listen to a single word; I'm master here!"

With that he vanished, and I flew to the door and locked it.

I now thought I would have some fun, so, as Monsieur B. had declined my attempts at an amicable restitution of the room, I decided to take him at his word, and allow—nay, compel him to take it by main force, as he had said he would. I handed baby to the servant, and sat down again, little terrified Henry asking me what it all meant.

I knew that my husband was going to send over an orderly to ascertain how I was being treated, and that Mr. B. was not aware of this, so I turned to the window, like Fatima, to ask the trembling nurse, "Sister Anne, Sister Anne, do you see anybody coming?" and—beheld Mr. B., who jumped through the window accompanied by the Kafir youths, who shook in their shoes I was going to say, but I must rather say shook in their soles at my unexpected defiance of the great man!

They now began throwing my furniture out of the window in the most careless way, B. inciting them to do so, and almost out of his mind with fury.

I now went up to the enemy. He paused for a second, and then opening the door shouted, "Now go, go, go! or I'll have you carried out. By —— I will."

This was too much to bear! No, I thought; these Kafir gentlemen shall see mind conquer matter, and the weak woman leave this room when she chooses, and not before! I now had my opportunity. Mr. B. stood at the door waiting for me to pass out. I affected an air of submission, and apparently leaving the room, approached the door; but, just as he was about to close it, suddenly faced round, and looked him full in the face with the question, "Mr. B., are you a Christian?"

"At the same moment I compelled myself to place my hand upon the wrist of his grimy, unpleasant arm, the sleeves of which were turned up for the energetic work he imagined he had to perform! Oh! what a look he gave my hand! For one instant I saw him try to dash it away, but he did not quite venture upon that, and now the quiet hand seems to calm him.

"Are you a Christian, Mr. B.?" I repeated, never relaxing my fingers from that wriggling wrist!

Mr. B. looked up; Mr. B. looked down,—gave a side-long glance at my poor little hand, and another at the Kafir boys, who were now grinning and giggling at the master before whom they had so recently trembled. The poor man saw he had made a mistake!

"Weel, marm! "he drawled, "I humbly hope I am a sincere Christian, and—"

I interrupted: "Of course you are! I have always had the greatest respect for you, Mr. B.; but—may I ask if you think the mode you have chosen either a Christian or a gentlemanly way of asking me to retire from this apartment?"

I now relaxed my hold, and seeing the storm was over, told him I was perfectly aware that the room belonged to him for the present, but that I should be glad to have a few moments' conversation with him, and as I could no longer offer him a chair, would he be kind enough to allow me to sit down for a moment on a box, (which had been too heavy to be thrown out.)

The Kafir youths looked on amazed as they saw the "ramping, raging" lion of a few minutes before, sit down as "meek as a lamb," to listen patiently and respectfully to the sermon which I proceeded to administer. And now I had some amusement. The fame of his fury had gone the rounds of the establishment, and crowds who had assembled at the windows to see "the Lady" ejected, now had the mortification of beholding the Great Mogul, quiet, ashamed, and subdued, listen for as long as I chose to preach, to the description of the mistake he had made, and to the announcement that the orderly had meanwhile arrived, and before twenty-four hours were over he would have to account to my husband for his conduct!

He was now trembling all over, white as death, and the perspiration was dripping off his brow in clammy drops, which seemed to carry away all his courage with it. I thought it only kind to end his misery, so I now summoned the Kafir boys, and requested them to carry to my other rooms the necessary furniture, &c., leaving on the best possible terms with Mr. B., who gaspingly ejaculated, "You are not in the least like any lady I ever saw in my life before!"

I now walked to my room to indulge the laughter I could no longer restrain; the crowd dividing right and left, and evidently thinking I was a "Witch Doctor" at the very least. But I must calm my shaken nerves, and receive the young Irish orderly whom my husband's note directs me "to pet to my, heart's content." I have never seen him before, but my husband has spoken so warmly of him, that I am prepared to like him very much, and the first look at his bright, ingenuous Irish face satisfies me my husband's eulogium is well deserved.

A few words are sufficient for "Mr. Burke," as I shall call him; and without waiting even for a mouthful of food or a glass of wine, back he dashes to my husband, fifteen miles away. The rest of the day is spent rearranging our two original rooms. I lie down to rest, but, too excited to sleep, take a book and begin to read. It is nearly midnight, when I hear my husband's signal whistle, and in another moment the sash is raised from without, and Edward springs lightly through the window, (it seems the fashionable mode of entrance today), and informs me that the horsewhip he holds in his hand is intended for Mr. B.'s benefit in the morning!

His horse is knee-haltered outside, and we give him some of our "*mealies*;" and now I thank my husband for his chivalry, which I greatly appreciate, and heartily enjoy the joke of his actually sleeping in the house while Mr. B. imagines him to be many, many miles away. I need hardly say I induced Edward to look at the bright side of the affair, but he nevertheless demands a couple of apologies, which poor B. humbly writes next morning; after which the affair is over, and poor, dear *Jack in Office* murmurs faintly that he "heartily wishes they had never made him 'Commandant,' that he do; for it gives him no peace, day nor night." (I need scarcely add that I bear no malice to the worthy man, and merely recall the episode to show we had some small excitement even in that dull life!)

CHAPTER 29

Entrance into Toleni

And now my husband tells me that the Gcaikas have invaded the Transkei, and that it being no longer possible to continue his work at Toleni, he intends to come and stay with us at Blythwood for a little while. So a couple of days after he arrives; escort, wagon, seven horses—quite a little cavalcade! and henceforth we part no more. Mr. B., who is now all smiles and civility, makes over two, upper rooms to my husband, and one is converted into an office, while the other accommodates the police, whom Mr. B. is evidently glad to have, to assist in defending the place. And now the barricades must be put up again, (not over my windows though, I never had them for a single day,) and the families who had so gladly gone home, again seek shelter at Blythwood. And now, alas! returns the noisy set banished by Captain Dearie; B. and his family occupy Mrs. Eustace's room; the whole tone of the place is changed, and Blythwood is no longer a fit place for a lady.

My husband employs himself with office work, and goes over constantly to Toleni, pushing on the work whenever he gets a chance of a few labourers; but now he is seized with serious illness, and there is no doctor to be had! At last, in despair, I take the responsibility to send off an orderly to Ibéka to beg and implore Colonel Eustace to induce the authorities to allow one of the military doctors to come over, at any expense; as I do not know what more to do for my husband, who gets weaker every day.

My anxiety was great; but, strange to say, my husband's ill-ness took a favourable turn, and he began to get better. It was fortunate that he did; as though I had despatched the messenger on Friday afternoon, the doctor did not arrive at Blythwood until the following Tuesday night, owing to a complication of adventures and disasters! (How would you like that, my friends at home, when those dear to you are suffering, and you see them failing for want of medical aid?)

The invalid is convalescent when the good doctor arrives, but the latter gentleman remains as our guest until the following day, and we also pay him six guineas, which is not much, considering his loss of time at Ibéka. The worthy doctor's visit is not wasted, for we have to consult him about a domestic event which is expected shortly. He strongly advises our coming down to the camp at Ibéka, as I have neither doctor nor nurse near Blythwood.

"I will take every care of your wife, and she will get on splen-didly in the fresh air!"[1] I naturally shrank from the bustle and stir of a large military camp, and my husband objected to tent life for me; so, hoping something may "turn up," we banish the idea; but it takes root in my brain to bear fruit hereafter.

And now a third consultation takes place, and the kind, good doctor for the first time opens our eyes to the fact, that our invalid child is not very long to remain with us! He most kindly promises to allow us wine, cod-liver oil, and other things needed for the darling from the hospital stores, and an orderly returns with him to fetch them from Ibéka. I will not,—cannot enter-tain, the fearful shadow which this visit casts over our home, but all the same, henceforward make baby my sole charge, and cling to him with a tenacity which only the fingers of Death have power to loose.

And now with the prospect of the arrival of a little stranger in our family, and with the shadow of death hanging heavily over our infant invalid, it is small wonder if my thoughts turn long-

---

1. Our house at Idutywa was now occupied by a magistrate, Mr. T. Merriman, son of the Bishop of Graham's Town.

ingly to a home of our own; even if that home be but a tent! Confusion, noise, and vulgarity reign supreme at Blythwood; and there is not an hour, hardly a moment in the day, in which we are not exposed to some annoyance.

At last, on Saturday, the 23rd of February, my husband rides away to Toleni; people imagine he will be absent several days, and the scene of confusion attains a climax which makes me resolve that before next Saturday arrives, I will sleep in a tent; on the "*veldt*;" anywhere,—anywhere,—to escape from this discomfort. I bottle up my wrath until my husband arrives, and finding he is tired out after his long journey, merely tell him I am quite happy, for I have thought of a plan which will meet all our difficulties, and which shall be unfolded to him on the morrow.

He laughingly pretends he is dying with impatience to hear it, and I am consumed with equal impatience to unfold it, but in the colonies, some daily duties must be attended to on a Sunday almost as much as on any other morning, and it is four o'clock in the afternoon before, having sent the children out and prepared afternoon tea; we sit down for a comfortable chat.

I relate the experiences of the preceding day, and suggest that, as my husband's work is at Toleni, where there is a hospital camp, we should proceed there immediately; thus ensuring greater quiet than at Ibéka (as only a small detachment of the 24th is at Toleni), and giving my husband the opportunity of continuing his work in the best way possible. Charmed with the idea, my husband at once adopts it, and concentrates his mental energy upon the task of leaving as quickly as possible. This is not very easy.

However, wonders can be done when people put their hearts into the matter, and on the following Thursday, the 28th of February, 1878, we left Blythwood at last, (having arrived there on the 29th of September, 1877,) so I fulfilled my vow not to remain another week there. But what a journey awaits us! Nothing but sunshine had been seen for weeks, but at the very moment of leaving Blythwood so violent a thunder storm burst suddenly over us, that we were all drenched in simply running from the house to the wagon, and soon the mattress on which we reclined, and everything about us, was soaked as if we lay in a pool. Unfortunately too, the man from whom we hired oxen (to supplement the Government supply), did not arrive until so late in the day, that though the poor children and I had been ready since nine o'clock in the morning, we did not start till five in the afternoon. (I wish Sir Isaac Newton had tried South Africa; if he had kept his temper there, I should indeed think him a saint). However, the worst of the storm was soon over, though small, fine rain continued for many hours, and we jogged along pretty comfortably until it got dark.

But now the road—wagon-track rather—passes over hills; and the wagon often bumps into holes, or crunches over large stones. Our little invalid becomes violently ill, and my old linen gown is soon only fit to throw away. Poor Henry is frightened at the dark and the shrieks and screams of the Kafirs, (for he is no longer the brave little hero of a year before; the terrible scenes through which the child has passed have caused a shock to the nervous system from which it may take years to recover), and, without a nurse, and in considerable suffering myself, I have enough to do to be patient.

At last my husband announces that we are on Toleni Hill, only a few minutes' distance from the accommodation-house where we intend to sleep that night. Vain hope! At this instant with an awful crash that seems to be rending the wagon into pieces, we descend into a frightful hole, and there we remain until daylight. The wagon is all on a slant, and the children and I are dashed violently against the side.

My husband rides on to the hotel with the wish,—I cannot say the hope,—of getting assistance, but returns alone with the following interesting items of intelligence.—First; the bedroom in which the poor children and I hoped to rest, is occupied by two ladies, who are not likely to leave for some time. (Oh, horror! Ladies at Toleni, just at this time of all others when I wanted to get away from everybody, and devote myself to our dying child!)—The whole of the rest of the house is occupied by No. 6, troop of mounted police, who are half dead with fatigue, and are lying on the bare floor,—anywhere about the shop and house. I "cannot possibly go there; the men are packed like herrings in a barrel." Mr. Hamilton and "Jack" Maclean are there; are "awfully sorry" for us, and Mr. Hamilton has sent me a glass of brandy and water.

"What comical comfort," I laugh; "would it were a cup of tea!" No chance of such a thing, so the babies and I divide the brandy and prepare to camp out. (I should explain that our escort had been left at Blythwood to bring over the horses, office-things, engineering instruments, and some furniture, &c.). My husband again departs, and this time finds a real, good Samaritan whose kindness I can never forget. He joyfully returns, saying that Mr. St. Leger L. (who has been my husband's deputy at Toleni), has been as good and kind as usual; that he is preparing cocoa and hot milk for the children, boiling eggs, and bringing bread to us, and that we shall have some breakfast in a few minutes.

"Breakfast! You don't mean to say it is tomorrow morning?" I reply.

"Not far off, old lady; so drink your grog and go to sleep." I am about to obey this affectionate, if inelegant direction, when kind Mr. St. Leger L. and his servant arrive, with a lantern and all sorts of luxuries, and we are soon having some nice supper, after which the children and I really do go to sleep. I always feel we owed that "forty winks" to Mr. Hamilton's brandy and water, which was not mixed on the Homoeopathic system!

We enjoyed our nap very much, but the awakening was not quite so agreeable. A lurch, a crunch, another mighty shock and effort; and the wagon has been hoisted out of the hole, and is ready to advance.—I hear the sound of a bugle; see a pretty, miniature, military camp, and at the same moment the troop of police is mounted in line, just on the point of departure.—The whole scene was enchanting! The beautiful hill-scenery shining through a delicate, silvery veil of mist which was tinted most exquisitely by the rising sun; the scarlet coats of our own "real,"

English soldiers, and the contrast presented by the dark uniform of the police,—all harmonized into a picture which I can never forget.

CHAPTER 30

Serious Anxiety

The wagon now advanced until it arrived at the hill which my husband had selected for our projected, camp life. This was a very beautiful spur or terrace, overlooking the valley of the Kei, and commanding as fine a view as could be found anywhere in the Transkei. We were sufficiently near to the trader's shop for convenience, and in proximity to the military camp in case of emergency, though separated from both by the high road, and quite far enough away to be disturbed by nothing that might occur at either place.

And now Edward told me that he had lent several of the tents to some police now stationed at Toleni, and that I had better take shelter in that occupied by Mr. St. Leger L., until he could put up one or two on the site selected for our own future camp. This did not sound attractive, but it was. preferable to facing the stylish ladies, fresh from England, who were now at the hotel; so I patiently submitted, and followed my husband as best I could, to the tent; which was in the very centre of the police camp. I tried to put on my boots, but they were so stiff from the continuous soaking they had undergone during the night that they could only be thrown away, so I walked across the soaking grass barefooted, and in the most dilapidated condition I have ever been in, in the whole course of my life.

My hair was hanging over my shoulders (not becomingly dishevelled as it would have been described in a novel, but twisted and tangled into frightful confusion). My dress was simply fit for a bonfire, and for nothing else in this world, and hat and veil were reduced to a state of shapeless pulp. However, I had nothing to regret, as all had been selected on account of their venerable age and antiquity, and their loss would be no affliction; the hair would soon recover itself, and my boots could be replaced by others close at hand, so I followed my husband merrily enough; the lovely sunshine cheering my heart and drying my garments in a most agreeable and practical manner.

We had had excellent servants at Blythwood, but they naturally objected to leaving their own neighbourhood in the present, unsettled condition of the country, so I had only one servant with me, who lived near Toleni, and was glad to be brought safely home. This girl was a stranger to baby, who did not like her at all. However, the poor darling enjoyed the fresh air and sunshine, and after taking some warm milk, was carried about on the "*veldt*," while Henry disappeared, attracted by the sight of the camp; and was taken possession of by the soldiers there, one nice serjeant amusing him most kindly for a long time.

My husband soon brought me a box of clothing, and I made my first toilet in a tent. And now an embarrassment, which had never occurred to me, presents itself for solution. What shall I put on?—I had prepared a thick morning-dress, but the atmosphere of the tent is so stifling that anything but muslin would suffocate me. I drag an old Jamaica gown out of the box, and sit down on the bed to brush my hair. I had hardly done so before a member of the police corps, imagining the tent is occupied by a bachelor, peeps in; smiles and nods at me till I nearly throw the hair-brush at his head, and departs; evidently thinking he has something amusing to relate to his comrades.

I try to smother my indignation, and endeavour to find some means of securing the tent from within. Edward returns to my assistance, and now all goes well, and I change the poor children's dress, and try to make them a little more clean and comfortable. My husband, anxious to get me away from the police, camp as rapidly as possible, now conducts us to "our" hill, where various members of the escort who had remained in charge of the "plant" there, are superintending Kafir labourers, who are putting up tents, digging trenches for drainage, and making a sod wall; as fast as black people ever will do anything.

Only one tent is up at present, and in this I see a table loaded with parcels of provisions; cups, saucers, knives, forks, and a teapot. Our first campfire is already blazing (as we had purchased some wood the previous day and tied it behind the wagon), and I am not disposed to grumble, as we are all very hungry, and must eat before we begin to evolve order from chaos. I must confess not only my own, but my husband's, patience was sorely tried when, at this moment, I find myself face to face with a lady in a dashing morning dress, who keeps me standing to talk about her trials and hardships at the hotel, (which I should have looked upon as a paradise of luxury) and inform me at parting she meant to come down again shortly to see how our "establishment" was getting on!

We had no front door to lock and no servants to say "Not at home," so my poor husband and I endeavour to bear this "last feather" as politely as possible; but I can say from the depths of my heart, that the last was by no means the least, in our burden of suffering.

After a hasty breakfast taken standing on the still soaking grass, I decide that the best thing I can do will be to get our blankets, mattresses, and pillows dried, and prepare a "nursery tent" for the children. So I put up a large clothes-rack and set to work; spending the entire morning in the open air, and thoroughly enjoying the sunshine. The day was simply perfect; the sun was not too hot; everything looked fresh and lovely after the rain; and the flowers seemed almost to spring up beneath my feet, which flew about in every direction until dinner-time.

The children were perfectly happy, amused by the busy scene about them, and I thought camp-life simply delightful! At midday, "we sat down to a tolerably tidy meal, and by sunset, when I had made the beds, put out the baths, and arranged our *karosses* and waterproofs on the ground in the two sleeping tents, things really began to look as if two more days' work would make us fairly comfortable.

We hoped some servants would come to be hired in a day or two, and meanwhile a Danish member of our escort had volunteered to take the cuisine off my hands, laughingly telling me it was not "proper" for "ladies to cook in camp." I slept like a top from sunset to sunrise, and for the first time enjoyed the never-to-be-forgotten luxury of sleeping in perfectly pure and fresh air. I discovered however, that my muslin dress had been about the worst attire I could possibly have selected for my day "on the *veldt*," especially after our late seclusion to the house at Blythwood. My neck and arms were completely skinned by the united exertions of sun and air, who had gone into partnership as doctors, and supplied me with a gratuitous, mustard poultice! I was not at all grateful for their exertions, but as I was not likely to wear evening dress in the Transkei, it did not much signify; though I carried the marks for many a day, and my "scars" were a lasting souvenir of our first day in camp.

The second day was not so agreeable.—The weather was perfect, but no servants appeared; the girl was grumbling and wanted to go home, and I found, to my dismay, that it was pay-day, (Saturday); so neither my husband, the escort, nor even the men, would be able to assist me in any way, and I could not unpack our boxes, as they were all at sixes and sevens, crowded into one tent, and I could not drag out even the smallest without a man's assistance. We all wanted clean clothes and a host of other things, and I felt especially anxious, as now a fresh terror presents itself. Suppose the new baby should take it into his head, (of course it will be a boy, all my sons are boys), to come and have a peep at the camp today, instead of waiting politely until everything is ready for his reception!

I dare not speak to my husband, for he is now on duty, and I would not disturb him for anything less than the enemy. Patience, Mrs. Prichard; sit still on the *veldt* and amuse yourself watching the scene, as circumstances are too much for you! Little Henry runs about, handing the pay to the men, and at last—after hours of sunshine, that I would have given worlds to have employed in emptying boxes and arranging our *bureaux*, Edward comes up to ask if lunch is ready?

"Oh! never mind lunch," I exclaim; "that must be despatched as rapidly as possible today."

Of course we both work our hardest all the afternoon, but have not accomplished more than half we ought to have ready, when alas! the sun goes down. For the very first time I sink into a chair, hoping to enjoy ten minutes' quiet and a cup of tea, before we set to work again.

My husband, looking up from his occupation of hammering down insecure tent-pegs, shouts to me the joyful intelligence, that he is "coming in a minute;" and I am just sighing out my gratitude for rest, and my admiration of the serenity and beauty of the landscape, which is being hushed to rest in the bosom of the Kei; when oh—! never! "Good gracious, Edward! there are two ladies and at least five or six gentlemen within two yards of you!"

So I have to rise and have all these people presented to me, and then drag myself about and exhibit our "establishment."

At last they leave, and I fly to my tent, and—soon I am the proud mother of another dear little son, who smiles at us most amiably, and does not seem at all aware that nothing is prepared for his reception, and that the box of baby linen has not yet made its appearance! So the little one must be dressed in borrowed plumes contributed by the darling—himself a baby still, (only fifteen months old,) who will so soon exchange these rough and unsuitable surroundings, for everything that is bright and beautiful above.

The four ensuing days can only be described by the one word, "*Kafoosalem!*" which my husband invariably applied to this most uncomfortable period of our camp life. The poor, distracted man—utterly out of his element, and bewildered in a maze of Babel and Babyland—vainly endeavoured to find the various garments required, which were all in far-distant boxes in a far-away tent! Without servants, without a nurse, without even a mother-in-law to help him, (what would not my husband have given for the appearance of that over-abused victim of popular prejudice?) he strove patiently from sunrise to sunset, and if the poor dear only succeeded in making us miserably uncomfortable, I am sure it was not his fault, though I could not help laughing at the very peculiar costumes in which he attired us!

Happily an old Kafir woman now appeared, and offered her services, while a very clever, bright-looking girl, who spoke English well, also came to our assistance, and took possession of the new baby, while poor little Granville was, alas! left to the tender mercies of the sulky individual who had accompanied us from Blythwood. And now I learn, not for the first time, how tender and kind men can be when one really needs their help. Our escort came forward gallantly; one made the gruel as if he had done nothing else all his life; another rode off to Cunninghame to beg Mrs. Ross for some of her delicious butter; a third went to forage for chickens in order to supply our little invalid with suitable nourishment, and a fourth devoted the Sunday to amusing our poor little eldest son, who seemed now "Nobody's Baby."

Unfortunately, violent storms of rain now set in and lasted for four days and nights; and no one but Mrs. Hutchinson, and other ladies who have really lived in camp, can form the smallest idea of the addition this rain proved to our sufferings. My own mind, too, was distracted with anxiety about little Granville. They would not let me see him, and I felt sure this was a bad sign! Meanwhile the rain descended, my husband went and came, and *Kafoosalem* reigned supreme!

On the fifth day, the glorious sunshine again appeared; and, longing to put everything in order, and resume the care of my poor, neglected children, I entreated Edward to carry me out, bed and all, to breathe the fresh air. He gladly complies with my request, as the tent is by this time four days deep in mud; and every officer who has been long under canvas knows what that means. The air revived me, and I lay under an umbrella, amusing myself watching the men who were now engaged in looping up the sides of the tent to dry it, and taking away wheelbarrow after wheelbarrowful of mud and sodden grass. The ground was now carefully scraped, swept, and left to dry; and we took care the same thing should be done immediately after to the nursery tent. And now I turn to look at a pretty scene on the terrace of the hill. A friend of Selina's from Mr. Ross's mission-station has relieved guard, sulky Maria having departed; and I now see the two young nurses, with their slim, graceful figures clad neatly in European costume, walking up and down the terrace, our two babies in their arms; little Henry running on to gather flowers for his brothers, and clapping his hands for joy that the rain is over. And now the girls, in their own enjoyment of the sunshine, begin to sing most melodiously some of the dear old English hymns that seem to take one straight away home in an instant.

Our little invalid smiles with pleasure, raises his pretty head, and begins to sing! The darling could not speak yet, and I was lost in amazement, as I heard his sweet, clear voice rise in harmonious tones and almost heavenly accents, upon the morning air. I fancied it was an omen of returning health and strength, and little knew it was the song of the dying swan;, the last faint flicker of the flame; and that even now, angels were on their way to bear my birdie home.

After the walk was over I managed to crawl to the children's tent to see our little invalid properly dressed and washed, and now I see for the first time the frightful change that has taken place during those four days. Oh, how they have neglected him! My darling is being starved to death!!

And now I pray,—nay, all but demand, supernatural strength to nurse and tend the little skeleton from whom others shrink in selfish terror. My new baby is apparently strong and well; he must wait for his mother's love until Granville is safe,—one way or the other! All that day I stand upon the *veldt*, for Heaven has heard my prayer, and fierce, fresh life seems to thrill through every vein and strengthen every nerve, as I think of my child's approaching battle with death.—We engage a clever, active woman to starch and iron and help me to put things tidy; that is to say, tidy enough for this time of emergency; prettiness, and the order I should like about my home, must wait for many a long day yet.

"Never mind my dress; anything will do for me; something that will wash—a white dress if possible; so that when my child awakes in heaven he will think the angel near him is his mother."

All day long I sit beside his bed, or hold him on my lap outside the tent that he may breathe the pure air; my pretty infant can only come to me occasionally, when Granville sleeps; for he is furious at the sight of his little brother and beats him fiercely away with his feverish hand. Thus a whole month passes away; visitors come and go daily, officers pass up and down, amongst them our kind, old friend Captain (now Major) Robinson, whose sympathy seems ready and sincere.

The 24th depart, and are succeeded by some Pullen Rangers; troops march through Toleni; some imperial, many irregular, and all this time I scarcely stir from my darling's side; or dress, or eat, or sleep. But now warm, genial weather seems to put fresh life into the child, and one wild, wicked moment I vow that death shall never snatch him from me until he has struck me down first.—And now, on Sunday night, the 7th of April, my warning comes! I fall asleep and dream that my little invalid is lying in my arms, when a veiled figure approaches; and, in tearing my child from my clasping arms, crushes me with its awful weight. I awake trembling and weeping, and know I must submit.—That very day a bitter dust-storm shakes down our tents and chills his little life away.

CHAPTER 31

A Child's Funeral

As I go to fetch some milk from the "mess" tent, I fall prone to the very earth in sheer physical exhaustion, having met with an injury in nursing Granville. They bring a little camp-bedstead, lay me gently on it; and never again do I gaze upon my darling's large, blue eyes or see a look of love upon that patient face. All day I am nearly unconscious, but at midnight I call to my husband—who does not reply; for he sees that our darling is passing away.—Another relapse into unconsciousness, and now I am awake again, quite awake, and—something is in the tent! Ah me, it was the touch of an angel's wing as he bore my child away.

All night long we watched; and, in the early morning, a messenger goes to good Mrs. Ross, the wife of the honest and upright missionary at Cunningham. He returns with lovely rosebuds for my angel-child, and a gentle note of tender sympathy for me. And in the grey, chilly, winter afternoon, a little procession passes through our camp to give almost military honours to my little hero.

Our own dear escort carry him reverently to the little grave prepared for him on the mountain side, and there the solemn service is read, and little Henry sees his brother laid tenderly to rest, by the kind hands which have often played with the darling, and whose sympathetic help is now so sweet a solace in the midst of our deep grief! [1] As the white coffin passes my tent, I

---

1. I can never thank them enough—we felt it very much.

dare not weep, for now our other babe has the first claim, and no selfish indulgence of my anguish must deprive him of his rights. I cannot yet rise from my bed, and when I .do so at the end of a week, it is a weary, broken-hearted woman who comes forth to face her clouded future, and who looks back upon the merry creature who laughed her way into Toleni, as upon a lost friend whom one will never meet again.

And now little Henry takes his place as my eldest son, and comforts me as no one else can.—He sits beside me for hours, kissing and stroking my hand; and when I totter from one tent to the other, he walks beside me, that I may support myself by resting my hand upon his shoulder. For a great change has fallen over me; all my energy seems to have gone with my vanished strength, and I sit in the midst of disorder that would have worried me to death three months before; uncomfortable at it, and vaguely annoyed by it; but patiently hoping next week I shall feel stronger, and then I can soon put everything to rights. For I really am not very strong, and it is many weeks before I can even go to see my child's grave, and that will be my first pilgrimage. For in the distance a cairn is rising to mark the spot, and when it is completed, a lofty cross will surmount the whole; to serve as a memorial of the patient little darling whose life here was one weary day of pain!

But I must rouse from my reverie, for my husband is begging me to come and "look at the Dungeon," and I must affect an interest I do not feel, for his sake. Now to explain;.—ever since the first dust-storm we have had such a succession of furious gales, that our tents afford but scanty shelter; some are tearing into ribbons, and we must seek some other dwelling as fast as we can. One day my husband begins digging a hole in the hill, and informs me that I am going to live in this hole some day!

"Live in it!.—Die in it, you mean!" I incredulously reply.

My husband, however, knows what he is about, and at last completes a gigantic excavation, which assumes the dimensions and shape of a long, deep room. Kafir women are now summoned, who smear the walls and floor with *dargha* (dried manure), and work up the surface with crushed ant-heap. This process of "papering" is not very agreeable, and we suffer from nausea and headache the whole time. Once dry, however, it is all right.

After a proper interval, the same women stain the surface with red ochre, which is afterwards white-washed. A wooden door and window are now added, (as the upper part of the dungeon is the sod wall of our camp), and a canvas cover is put over the whole by way of a roof. A procession of women carry thither carpets and furniture one Saturday afternoon, and that night, the 4th May, we all sleep there for the first time.

The dimensions of our apartment seem almost palatial after the tents; we dine there by lamplight at a nice, good-sized table, and think the dungeon a great success. Next day is extremely warm; the sunshine throws such pretty tints through the canvas roof upon the crimson carpet and Swedish furniture, that I sit "like a lady" in a "book muslin gown," and write a *couleur-de rose* effusion to my Mother in England, describing the charms of life in a dungeon in terms almost calculated to make every reader turn pale with envy! I am washing my hands to remove the very numerous ink-stains with which my fingers are adorned, when I see something looking at me out of the pink wall.

"Ugh! oh! John, Selina, Somebody I come quick and take away this creature out of the wall!"

And I retreat to avoid seeing the unsightly worm which John gradually succeeds in removing. I now draw the beds farther away from the "pretty, pink wall "I had so gushingly described, and think it fortunate my letter is already on its way to cheer the anxious mother about her Crusoe-like daughter! I have engaged a Kafir maid, who is to come next day to assist in needlework, and run about for me, &c., as I am too weak to do much, and next morning sit down in peace and quiet to sew beside my maid, like a lady at home. Quiet!.—At this moment a furious and totally unexpected gust of wind, blows our roof off; while clouds of dust whirl down upon the neatly-arranged room, and make the whole place only fit for a chimneysweep.

We have to put aside our needlework, and return to the tents, which are blowing away in all directions, and it is the work of a day to put things to rights again. A succession of dust-storms by day, and floods of rain at night, which deluge our beds, and make everything most dismal, convince us that the dungeon can scarcely be looked upon as anything but a temporary residence; and my husband now commences to erect a "Kafir Palace."

CHAPTER 32

"Under Orders for Home"

This is a work of time, and we do not go into quarters at the "Palace" until the 18th of June, after having slept under canvas since the 1st of March. Meanwhile various interesting events occur, among which I may note the arrival of the 24th Regiment at Toleni on Sunday, the 9th of June. Major Logan and Captain Austen came in the morning to ask my husband to help them about something or other, oxen, I think; and both were very kind to our little son Henry, who evidently admired the soldiers very much, particularly Major Logan, who had a red coat on!

I could not receive them myself, as my spirits were still quite unequal to the effort of meeting any but old friends, but I had a little peep at them out of the Dungeon, and quite appreciated their kindness to our little son. In the afternoon, my husband persuaded me to walk up to the hotel to visit a lady who was staying there, and as Captain Austen and Major Logan did the same thing, we met them again. Captain Austen's quiet, gentle manner pleased me very much, and I was greatly distressed when I heard that he and others whom we had met had perished on the field of Isandlhana.

They were in good spirits, as they were under orders for home, and pitied us for being compelled to remain in the Transkei, as much as we envied them for leaving it. How little I guessed, as Captain Austen held open the door for me as I left, that it was I who would see dear old England again, while he would find a hero's grave in Zululand! Another day, Lord Chelmsford (then

General Thesiger) and his staff, made a commotion in our very small world. My husband went down to pay his respects, [1] and our friend Major Robinson, dined and remained that night with us; but I need hardly say our recent loss was sufficient reason to prevent my wishing anyone else to visit us so soon.

I fear the major fared but badly, as poor John, our Kafir chef, only knew how to cook about three things at that time, and had yet to acquire the noble art, in which he afterwards improved so rapidly! However, our guest made kind allowance for all deficiencies, and was so amusing that he made me laugh for the first time since my darling's death.

---

1. The commander-in-chief at the Cape is also lieutenant-governor of the Colony.

Conclusion: God save the Queen

Our next, small excitement was on Saturday, the 29th of June, when the 90th Regiment passed through Toleni, [1] and encamped for Sunday's rest on a hill about half a mile away. My husband told me they were going to bring their band, and this exciting piece of intelligence kept me on the *qui-vive* all the morning. I could resist the general, I could resist the 24th, but I could not resist a band!! So I sat sewing with my hat on, ready to dash out of the "palace" at a moment's notice. In vain John informed me "lunch" was ready, and the cutlets were "turning black!"—Who could think of mutton and music in the same breath?

Out I flew, as my husband shouted "Here they come!" through the open door of the hut. John snatched up his cutlets and hastily followed me, and we abandoned the Public Works Camp in the most disgraceful manner. And now we stand quietly at the side of the road to see the beautiful spectacle. How our hearts beat and our pulses thrill, as the stately column passes grandly along; for are not these our own countrymen, come to defend us with their latest breath; and do they not bring with them a breath of home and all that is most dear?

As the band approaches, I cannot help whispering, "Oh, if they would but play!" and lo! at the same instant, as if by magic, a most enchanting air—so soft, so sweet, so exquisitely in harmony with the clear atmosphere, the blue sky, and the magnificent scenery—steals upon one's ear, and dissolves us all into tears. But now we reverently salute the Queen's colours, and—

---

1. On their way overland to Natal.

feeling I can bear no more I run away,—and wish all their foes, may do "that same"! We now return to John and the cutlets, which disappear; but whether they were brown, black, or white, is a matter of the utmost indifference to us all!

With the exception of dust-storms and. visitors, both events of almost daily occurrence, nothing important happened in our little household until the 18th July, when an interesting but impromptu ceremony was performed there. I had been ill, and was only dressing in time for lunch, when I heard a voice asking in very gentle tones, "Are there any babies here to christen?"

"Yes, yes, Plenty!" I exclaim in my nervousness (from the other side of the partition-wall); "please be kind enough to sit down; my husband will be here in a moment, and we hope you will stop to lunch."

(I haven't the faintest idea whom I am addressing, but consider myself a connoisseur in voices, and know it is all right, and that the unknown is a gentleman an Englishman, too, I think.) My husband now appears, and informs me that the Rev. ——will be kind enough to christen baby immediately, and has gone to fetch his surplice. I send for baby, hastily put a pretty, English, white frock over his Transkei garments; request "Mr. Burke" to do proxy for an absent godfather (Major Elliot); snatch the bread out of the cake-basket, and put water into it by way of a font; summon the servants (who are excited and interested), to act congregation; and the ceremony begins. I am not in a devotional mood, and cannot feel as one ought, at a moment's notice.

Baby is a dreadfully old baby, and doesn't behave at all properly, and at first I am rather inclined to laugh! However, the beautifully simple service touches my heart, and brings back thoughts of our lost darling and of dearly-loved friends who assisted at his christening! Tears gather in my eyes as I think of the woman I so dearly love, and from whom circumstances have divided me; and now I am quiet enough, as the good clergyman blesses the poor little child who came to us in a tent, and without a single comfort about him! "Bernard Elliot;" yes: that name will recall family associations, and the kind friend who has been so closely connected with our life in the Transkei;—and now the good clergyman has gone, and we are receiving other visitors who have no idea what has just occurred.

A Kafir hut is a queer place for a christening;—but I don't think I have described our little cabin, and must do so before I say farewell to my friends. It is exactly like any other hut, only very much larger; being fully thirty feet in diameter. It is divided by a partition into two large, semi-circular rooms; one of which is of course our bedroom and the other our sitting-room. Into the centre of this partition-wall is built our range, from the dear little kitchen at Idutywa, and our chimney is a telegraph-pole, which my husband sweeps every other day!! But if I begin to talk about our life in a Kafir hut, I may just as well commence another volume at once, for every day there was an amusing or pathetic episode, and the patience of my readers would be exhausted.

One, however, I may mention; reserving all others for a future occasion.

The Kafir belles look really picturesque in their native dress, which is perfectly modest and dignified, and certainly the best thing they could possibly wear on the breezy highlands of the Transkei, where they are scorched by tropical sunshine one moment and exposed to an icy blast the next. But in their caricatures of European costume they are simply ridiculous, especially as nearly all their dresses are sent out secondhand from ladies' wardrobes at home; and I remember the difficulty with which I kept my gravity when a favourite domestic paraded up and down in the wilderness, clad in the thinnest of transparent, black grenadines, which had once been a really pretty, evening-dress for a "blonde," but transformed into the sole garment of a brunette on a windy winter's day, looked the very personification of unsuitable finery!

The only redeeming feature in the affair was the beaming face of the happy wearer, who was so charmed with her dress that I really had not the heart to undeceive her. However, I ventured to present her with an aged satin skirt, with which she was perfectly enchanted; and by the addition of a black under-bodice and a few other necessaries managed to make her presentable for that day!

However, Miss Lizzie did not altogether appreciate the idea of wearing black satin under her dress, so next day, on a blazing hot morning, I found her sitting in the dust-hole, the centre of a circle of envious but admiring lady friends, with her newly-acquired treasure put on outside her cotton working-gown, and, I need scarcely add, that by the end of the day, it was so much injured by this unexpected treatment, that I almost regretted having interfered at all, and felt tempted to let them all convert themselves into scarecrows, *a piacere*.

My failing health soon rendered a trip to England necessary, and as peace was declared, and the very last remnant of a redcoat had vanished from the Transkei, we were now at liberty to think of ourselves. As cold weather would not be at all likely to benefit me, we decided to pass the winter months in the Tropics, Egypt, and the Mediterranean, hoping to reach England in the spring of 1879. My husband thought it not unlikely that *en route* we might find some climate which would recruit my health and suit him professionally at the same time.

We left Toleni camp on the 25th of September, and arrived safely at Zanzibar on the 15th of November, 1878, taking with us kind wishes and regrets from the friends left behind, and papers from my husband's official chief, testifying to the services he had rendered the colony, and fully explaining the reason of our departure. Armed with these papers we steamed away for Zanzibar.—And here I will rest for the present, tendering my sincere thanks to my patient readers, and offering very grateful remembrances to the friends at Zanzibar who gave us so kind a welcome! (I need scarcely say, we were not supposed to have any foes there.) And now *adieu*; but as I consider myself quite a little soldier, having been close to the front all through a campaign, during which I suffered many a wound, let my last words be:-
The Queen!